Collins

真正上海数学

Real Shanghai Mathematics

6.1

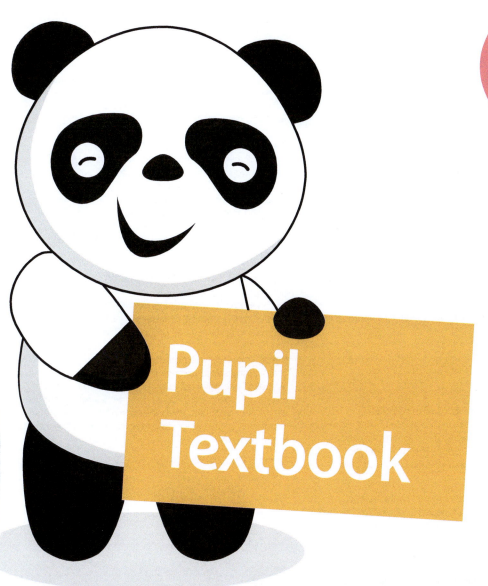

Pupil Textbook

世纪出版

上海教育出版社
SHANGHAI EDUCATIONAL
PUBLISHING HOUSE

MIX
Paper from responsible sources
FSC™ C007454

This book is produced from independently certified FSC™ paper to ensure responsible forest management.

For more information visit: **www.harpercollins.co.uk/green**

William Collins' dream of knowledge for all began with the publication of his first book in 1819. A self-educated mill worker, he not only enriched millions of lives, but also founded a flourishing publishing house. Today, staying true to this spirit, Collins books are packed with inspiration, innovation and practical expertise. They place you at the centre of a world of possibility and give you exactly what you need to explore it.

Collins. Freedom to teach.

Collins
An imprint of HarperCollins*Publishers*
The News Building
1 London Bridge Street
London
SE1 9GF

Browse the complete Collins catalogue at
www.collins.co.uk

The educational materials in this book were compiled in accordance with the course curriculum produced by the Shanghai Schools (Pre-Schools) Curriculum Reform Commission and 'Maths Syllabus for Shanghai Schools (Trial Implementation)' for use in Primary 6 First Term under the nine-year compulsory education system.

These educational materials were compiled by the head of Shanghai Normal University, and reviewed and approved for trial use by Shanghai Schools Educational Materials Review Board.

The writers for this book's educational materials are:
Editors-in-Chief: Qiu Wanzuo, Part II, Huang Hua

Guest Writers (Listed by Chinese character strokes in surname):
Zhang Yun, Ke Xinli, Xia Yingping, Xu Xiaoyan, Huang Hua et al.

For the English edition:

Primary Publishing Director: Lee Newman
Primary Publishing Managers: Fiona McGlade, Lizzie Catford
Editorial Project Manager: Mike Appleton
Editorial Manager: Amanda Harman
Editorial Assistant: Holly Blood
Managing Translator: Huang Xingfeng
Translators: Cai Yufeng, Chen Yilin, Huang Chunhua, Ling Yujie, Xu Chengyi, Xu Huijing, Xu Yiwen, Yao Danting, Zhang Mingzhu, Zhang Yunji, Zhao Yaming, Zheng Shuting
Lead Editor: Tanya Solomons
Proofreaders: Joan Miller, Vivienne Church
Cover artist: Amparo Barrera
Designer: Ken Vail Graphic Design
Production Controller: Sarah Burke
Printed and bound by CPI Group (UK) Ltd, Croydon, CR0 4YY

Photo acknowledgements
The publishers wish to thank the following for permission to reproduce photographs. Every effort has been made to trace copyright holders and to obtain their permission for the use of copyright materials. The publishers will gladly receive any information enabling them to rectify any error or omission at the first opportunity.

All images with permission from Shanghai Century Publishing Group.

Contents

Unit Three: Ratio and proportion   76

Unit Four: Circles and sectors   107

Unit One
Divisibility of integers

Dylan is helping to decorate his family's new house. The floor of the living room is a rectangle with length 6 metres and width 4.8 metres. Dylan wants to use complete square tiles to cover the whole living room floor. The tiles in the shop come in four sizes: 30 × 30, 40 × 40, 60 × 60, 80 × 80 (units: cm²). Dylan wants to choose the largest size he can. Which size should he choose?

I'm Dylan. I would choose size 80 × 80 because the bigger the tile, the more beautiful the floor will be.

I'm Poppy. I would choose size 30 × 30, so that I could just use whole tiles to cover the floor.

I'm Emma. I would choose size 40 × 40, so that I could still just use whole tiles to cover the floor but they are a bit bigger.

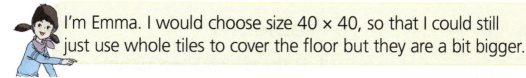

Are Dylan, Poppy and Emma correct? After you have learned the mathematics in this unit, you will be able to solve the problem for yourself.

Section One: Integers and divisibility
1.1 Integers and the meaning of divisibility

We often need to count objects, such as the number of eggs or the number of goats...

The numbers we use for counting, such as 1, 2, 3, 4, 5, ... are called **positive integers**. We can use zero when there is 'no object' and also to represent fixed values for some measured quantities, such as zero degrees Celsius.

Putting the minus sign (–) before positive integers such as 1, 2, 3, 4, 5, ... gives us numbers such as –1, –2, –3, –4, –5, ..., which are called **negative integers**. Zero is neither positive nor negative. These are ideas that you have learned previously and you will learn more about in the future.

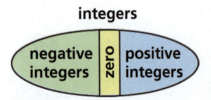

Zero and the positive integers form the set of all **natural numbers**. The positive integers, zero and the negative integers form the set of all **integers**.*

How many natural numbers are there altogether?

? **Problem 1**

1. Is there a smallest natural number?

2. Is there a greatest integer?

*Unless described otherwise, the integers used in this unit are all positive integers.

Think!

15 pupils take part in the summer activities. They want to divide into small groups, each with the same number of pupils, to do the activities. How can they divide themselves up?

If we divide equally into 3 groups, 15 ÷ 3 = 5, there are 5 people in each group.

If we divide equally into 5 groups, 15 ÷ 5 = 3, there are 3 people in each group.

Why can't we divide into 2 groups or 4 groups?

 # Observation

The dividends and divisors in these two sets of number sentence cards are all integers. Are there any differences in the results of the operations on them?

1.

24 ÷ 2 = 12

21 ÷ 3 = 7

84 ÷ 21 = 4

2.

6 ÷ 5 = 1.2

17 ÷ 10 = 1.7

35 ÷ 6 = 5 r 5

The quotients of the number sentences in the first group are all integers and the remainders are zero.

The quotients of the number sentences in the second group are all decimals, or the numbers do not divide exactly.

When we divide integer a by integer b, if the quotient is an integer and the remainder is zero, we can say that a is exactly divisible by b or that b divides exactly into a.

In the set of number sentences in the first group, 24 is divisible by 2, 21 is divisible by 3 and 84 is divisible by 21; we can also say that 2 divides exactly into 24, 3 divides exactly into 21 and 21 divides exactly into 84.

But in the set of number sentences in the second group, 6 is not divisible by 5, 17 is not divisible by 10 and 35 is not divisible by 6; we can also say that 5 cannot divide exactly into 6, 10 cannot divide exactly into 17 and 6 cannot divide exactly into 35.

Example   Which dividend is divisible by the divisor?

$$10 \div 3 \qquad 48 \div 8 \qquad 6 \div 4$$

Solution

$10 \div 3 = 3$ r 1

$48 \div 8 = 6$

$6 \div 4 = 1.5$

So the number sentence where the dividend can be divided by the divisor is $48 \div 8$.

? Problem 2

$2.6 \div 1.3 = 2$, so can you say that 2.6 can be divided exactly by 1.3?

Remember the conditions for exact division.
1. The divisor and the dividend are both integers.
2. The dividend is divided exactly by the divisor, the quotient is an integer and the remainder is zero.

Practice 1.1

1. **Write each number in the correct oval. Each number may go in one, two or none of the ovals.**

   $12, -7, 0, 0.4, -23, \dfrac{3}{4}, 91, -8.75$

   positive integers   **negative integers**   **integers**

2. Read what Dylan and Emma say. Are they right?

2.5 can be divided exactly by 5.

0 is a whole number.

3. Look at each pair of numbers. If the first number can be exactly divided by the second number, put a '✓' in the brackets and if it can't, put a '✗'.

72 and 36	17 and 34	20 and 5	0.5 and 5
( )	( )	( )	( )
18 and 3	19 and 38	0.2 and 4	17 and 3
( )	( )	( )	( )

1.2 Factors and multiples

 ## Think!

Use 12 identical squares.

How many different ways can you arrange the squares to make a rectangle?

Write the length and width of each rectangle.

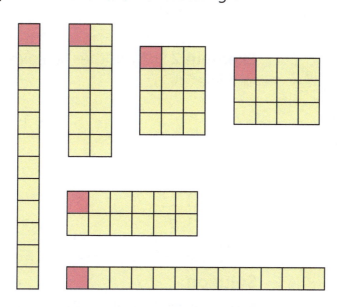

area	÷	length	=	width
12	÷	1	=	12
12	÷	2	=	6
12	÷	3	=	4
12	÷	4	=	3
12	÷	6	=	2
12	÷	12	=	1

1, 2, 3, 4, 6 and 12 all divide exactly into 12, so we say that they are the **factors** of 12 and 12 is a **multiple**.

Factors and multiples are interdependent.

→ If integer a can be divided exactly by integer b, then a is a **multiple** of b, and b is a **factor** of a.

Example 1 Write the factors of 16 and the factors of 13.

Solution

→ Factors of 16: 1, 2, 4, 8, 16

Factors of 13: 1, 13

The integers that can divide exactly into 16 are the factors of 16. First, find all the integers that can divide exactly into 16.
$16 ÷ 1 = 16$, $16 ÷ 16 = 1$, $16 ÷ 2 = 8$, $16 ÷ 8 = 2$, $16 ÷ 4 = 4$.

The smallest factor of any integer is 1 and the greatest factor is the integer itself.

All the integers that are divisible by 2 are multiples of 2. All the products of 2 and a positive integer such as 1, 2, 3, 4, 5… can be divided by 2.

Example 2 Write the multiples of 2 and the multiples of 5.

→ | 2 |

$2 \times 1 = 2$

| 2 | 2 |

$2 \times 2 = 4$

| 2 | 2 | 2 |

$2 \times 3 = 6$

....

Solution

Multiples of 2: 2, 4, 6, 8, 10, 12, 14…

Multiples of 5: 5, 10, 15, 20, 25…

How many multiples does an integer have? Does it have a greatest or smallest multiple? If it has, what is it?

An integer doesn't have a greatest multiple but the smallest multiple is itself.

 # Practice 1.2

1. Mark the multiples of 3 on this number line.

0 1 2 3 4 5 6 7 8 9 10 11 12 13 14 15 16 17 18 19 20 21 22 23 24 25 26 27

2. Read what Dylan and Emma say. Are they right?

 Because $4 \div 2 = 2$, 4 is the multiple and 2 is the factor.

A number doesn't have a smallest multiple.

3. Write each of these numbers in the correct oval(s).

2, 3, 4, 5 6, 12, 15, 18, 20, 24, 30, 60

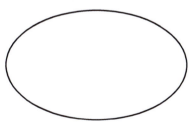

factors of 60

multiples of 6

4. Write all the factors of each of these numbers. Then write the three smallest multiples of each number.

12, 18, 30, 36

1.3 Numbers that are divisible by 2 or 5

Lots of the things we use come in pairs, for example shoes and chopsticks. If three people in Dylan's family are having a Chinese meal he lays out 6 chopsticks. If there are guests coming, then the number of chopsticks he lays out altogether must be a multiple of 2. The number of chopsticks is divisible by 2.

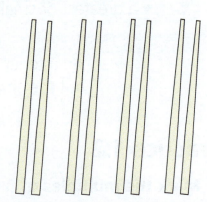

 ## Think!

What is special about a number that is divisible by 2?

 ## Observation

The numbers in the right-hand column of the diagram on the right are the first few multiples of 2. Each of these numbers is divisible by 2.

In the right-hand column, the multiples of 2 always end with 2, 4, 6, 8 or 0.

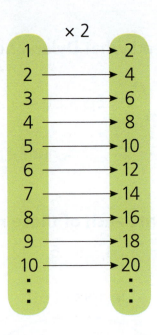

× 2

1	→	2
2	→	4
3	→	6
4	→	8
5	→	10
6	→	12
7	→	14
8	→	16
9	→	18
10	→	20

 ## Summary

Integers that have 0, 2, 4, 6 or 8 as the ones digit are divisible by 2.

Look at the page numbers in this book. Are all the left-hand page numbers exactly divisible by 2? Are all the right-hand page numbers exactly divisible by 2?

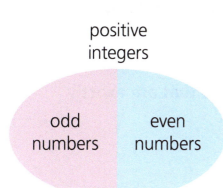

positive integers

odd numbers

even numbers

Integers that are exactly divisible by 2 are called **even numbers** and integers that are not exactly divisible by 2 are called **odd numbers**.

odd numbers	1, 3, 5, 7, 9, 11, 13…
even numbers	2, 4, 6, 8, 10, 12, 14…

Depending on whether or not they are exactly divisible by 2, positive integers can be separated into two sets: odd numbers and even numbers.*

 # Problems

1. **What is the property of the ones digits in odd numbers?**

2. **In the set of consecutive positive integers (except 1), can two adjacent numbers both be even or both be odd?**

Think!

What is the characteristic of integers that can be divided exactly by 5?

Observation

The integers in the right-hand column in the diagram on the right are the first few multiples of 5. All these integers are divisible exactly by 5.

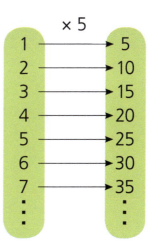

× 5

1 → 5
2 → 10
3 → 15
4 → 20
5 → 25
6 → 30
7 → 35

Summary

> Any integer that has 0 or 5 as the ones digit is divisible by 5.

*Here **odd numbers** and **even numbers** refer to positive odd numbers and positive even numbers. When the range of numbers is extended from positive integers to all integers, 0, −2, −4, −6 and so on are also even numbers, and −1, −3, −5 and so on are also odd numbers.

Practice 1.3

1. Look at these numbers. Which are odd numbers? Which are even numbers?

19, 32, 87, 10, 11, 153, 66, 45

2. Look at these numbers. Find the numbers that are exactly divisible by 5.

18, 27, 30, 44, 60, 102, 417, 375

3. Look at these numbers.

Find the numbers that are exactly divisible by both 2 and 5. Write them in the correct place on the diagram below.

12, 25, 40, 75, 80, 94, 105, 210

numbers that are exactly divisible by 2

numbers that are exactly divisible by 2 and 5

numbers that are exactly divisible by 5

Section Two: Prime factorisation

1.4 Prime numbers, composite numbers and prime factorisation

 Think!

How can you work out the factors of a positive integer? How many factors does a positive integer have?

It may have only one factor, such as the number 1.

It may have three factors, such as the number 4.

It may have two factors, such as the number 2.

Think: How many factors does each of these numbers have?

1, 2, 3, 4, 5, 6, 7, 8, 9, 10, 11, 12, 13, 14, …

Which number has just one factor? Which numbers have two factors? Which numbers have more than two factors?

 1?

A positive integer that has only two factors, which are 1 and itself, is called a **prime number**. If a number has more than two factors, including 1 and itself, it is called a **composite number**.

For example,

2, 3, 5, 7, 11, 13, … are prime numbers

4, 6, 8, 9, 10, 12, 14, … are composite numbers.

positive integers

prime numbers | 1 | composite numbers

1 is neither a prime number nor a composite number. So there are three sorts of positive integer: 1, prime numbers and composite numbers.

We can also test numbers by checking for exact division: 27 is divisible by 3. Therefore, as well as 1 and 27, 27 has a factor 3. So, 27 is a composite number. Similarly, 35 is divisible by 5, so 35 is also a composite number.

Example 1 Decide whether 27, 29, 35 and 37 are prime numbers or composite numbers.

Solution The factors of 27 are 1, 3, 9, 27.
The factors of 29 are 1, 29.
The factors of 35 are 1, 5, 7, 35.
The factors of 37 are 1, 37.

By looking at the number of factors of each of these numbers, we find that 29 and 37 are prime numbers, and 27 and 35 are composite numbers.

To decide whether or not a number less than 100 is a prime number, you can also refer to this table of prime numbers.

2	3	5	7	11	13	17	19	23
29	31	37	41	43	47	53	59	61
67	71	73	79	83	89	97		

Practice 1.4 (1)

1. Among the integers from 1 to 10,
   a. the odd numbers are ____ and the even numbers are ____.
   b. the prime numbers are ____ and the composite numbers are ____.

2. Are these statements correct?

A composite number has at least 3 factors.	All even numbers are composite numbers.

All odd numbers are prime numbers.	All positive numbers, except for prime numbers, are composite numbers.

3. Write these numbers in the correct places in the ovals.

11, 21, 31, 41, 51, 61, 71, 81, 91

prime numbers    composite numbers

4. Multiple choice

a. Among the positive numbers, 1 is (   ).

   A. the smallest odd number   **B.** the smallest even number

   C. the smallest prime number   **D.** the smallest composite number

b. Among the positive numbers, 4 is (   ).

   A. the smallest odd number   **B.** the smallest even number

   C. the smallest prime number   **D.** the smallest composite number

 Think!

How can you find the prime factors of 6, 28 and 60?

It's like the branches of a tree! This is called **branch decomposition** or **tree factorisation**.

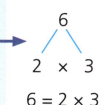

$6 = 2 \times 3$

$28 = 2 \times 2 \times 7$

$60 = 2 \times 3 \times 2 \times 5$
$\quad\;\; = 2 \times 2 \times 3 \times 5$

From the above examples, we can see that:

- every composite number can be written in the form of a product (multiplication) of several prime numbers

- a prime number that is a factor of the composite number is called a **prime factor of the composite number**

- the method of breaking a composite number into the product of its prime factors is called **prime factorisation**.

The divisors are written on the left, and this method of writing the division to find the quotient is called **short division**.

Example 2 Find the prime factors of 48, 35, 60.

Solution

```
2 | 48        5 | 35        2 | 60
  2 | 24          7           2 | 30
    2 | 12                      3 | 15
      2 | 6                        5
        3
```

$48 = 2 \times 2 \times 2 \times 2 \times 3; \; 35 = 5 \times 7; \; 60 = 2 \times 2 \times 3 \times 5$

Follow these steps to find the prime factors of a number by short division.

You can use mental calculation to do prime factorisation.

1. First, find a prime number that can divide into the composite number exactly. (We usually start with the smallest one, such as 2 or 3.) Divide it into your number.

Don't forget to check that every factor you choose is a prime number.

2. If the quotient is another composite number, use the same method to divide again. Repeat until the quotient is a prime number.

3. Now order the divisors and the final quotient, from smallest to greatest, and write them in the form of a multiplication of three or more numbers.

Using a calculator is called **machine calculation**. ⟶

We can also use a calculator to do prime factorisation. For example, using a calculator we get: $1334 \div 2 = 667$

Why would you divide by the prime number 2 again? ⟶

When we divide 667 by the prime numbers 2, 3, 5, 7, 11, 13, 17, 19 in turn, they all have remainders. This shows that they are not prime factors of 667.

However, dividing by the next prime number (23) $667 \div 23 = 29$, and 29 is a prime number.

So $1334 = 2 \times 23 \times 29$.

Practice 1.4 (2)

1. Prime factorisation of 42 gives $42 = 2 \times 21$.

If $A = 2 \times 3 \times 5 \times B$, and $B > 1$, B must be a prime factor of A.

Are Dylan and Poppy correct?

2. **Multiple choice**

   a. In the equation $4 \times 6 = n = 2 \times 2 \times 2 \times 3$,

   4 and 6 are (   ) of n,

   2 and 3 are (   ) of n.

   A. prime factors   **B.** prime numbers   **C.** factors

   D. composite numbers

b. Which is the correct prime factorisation of 24? (   )

A. 24 = 2 × 3 × 4   **B.** 24 = 2 × 2 × 2 × 3

C. 24 = 1 × 2 × 2 × 2 × 3   **D.** 24 = 2 × 2 × 6

3. Find the prime factors of each of these numbers.

21, 36, 56, 72, 81

1.5 Common factors and highest common factor

 Think!

On Tree Planting Day, the teacher takes 24 girls and 32 boys to the botanical gardens to plant trees. The teacher divides these pupils into groups of equal size, and the number of boys in every group is the same. How many groups can these 56 pupils be divided into, at most?

 The number of groups must divide exactly into both 24 and 32, so it must be a factor of 24 and of 32.

Factors of 24:   1, 2, 3, 4, 6, 8, 12, 24

Factors of 32:   1, 2, 4, 8, 16, 32

Common factors of 24 and 32 are 1, 2, 4 and 8.

factors of 24   factors of 32

3   6   1   2

12   24   4   8   16   32

common factors of 24 and 32

Therefore, the teacher can divide these pupils into a maximum of eight groups. And in each group, there are 3 girls and 4 boys.

A factor that divides exactly into two or more numbers is called a **common factor** of the numbers. The largest of these common factors is called the **highest common factor** of the numbers.

Example 1   Find all the common factors of 8 and 9, and then find their highest common factor.

Solution   The factors of 8 are 1, 2, 4 and 8. The factors of 9 are 1, 3 and 9.

8 and 9 have only one common factor, 1, so the highest common factor of 8 and 9 is 1.

> What is the difference between prime numbers and numbers that are relatively prime or co-prime?

> If two integers have only the common factor 1, the two numbers are called **relatively prime** or **co-prime**.

In Example 1, 8 and 9 are relatively prime.

1. Look at these five pairs of numbers:
   3 and 9, 4 and 9, 3 and 7, 7 and 14, 14 and 15
   Which pairs of numbers are relatively prime?

Example 2   Find the highest common factor of 18 and 30.

Solution

Method 1:   The factors of 18 are 1, 2, 3, 6, 9, 18.
            The factors of 30 are 1, 2, 3, 5, 6, 10, 15, 30.

The common factors of 18 and 30 are 1, 2, 3, 6.
The highest common factor of 18 and 30 is 6.

Method 2:   Use prime factorisation.

$$18 = 2 \times 3 \times 3$$
$$30 = 2 \times 3 \times 5$$

> Is there a better way to write these?

We can see that the common prime factors of 18 and 30 are 2 and 3, so 6 (the product of 2 and 3) is the highest common factor of 18 and 30.

Work out the highest common factor of a group of integers. As long as you multiply the prime factors that are common to all of them, the product is their highest common factor.

Method 3:   To be more efficient, you can also use short division.

```
2 | 18  30    Divide by the common prime factor 2.
  3 |  9  15   Divide by the common prime factor 3.
        3   5  Continue until the two quotients are relatively prime.
```

The highest common factor of 18 and 30 is 2 × 3 = 6.

Example 3 Work out the highest common factor of 48 and 60.

Solution

```
2 | 48  60    Divide by the common prime factor 2.
  2 | 24  30   Divide by the common prime factor 2 again.
    3 | 12  15  Divide by the common prime factor 3.
          4   5 Continue until the two quotients are relatively prime.
```

The highest common factor of 48 and 60 is 2 × 2 × 3 = 12.

Now let's go back to the question at the beginning of this unit.

To satisfy the condition that Dylan wants to use whole tiles, you need to be able to divide the length and width of the living room floor exactly by the length of the side of the tiles. First, make sure the length and width of the room and the length of the side of the tile are in the same units. Change them all to centimetres.

Then the length of a tile should be a common factor of 600 cm (the length of the room) and 480 cm (the width of the room). 30, 40 and 60 are common factors of 600 and 480, but 80 is not a common factor of 600 and 480. So if Dylan wants to choose the largest possible tiles, he should choose those that are 60 cm × 60 cm.

2. **a.** The highest common factor of 3 and 15 is _____.

   b. The highest common factor of 18 and 36 is _____.

   c. The highest common factor of 6 and 7 is _____.

   d. The highest common factor of 8 and 15 is _____.

In finding the highest common factors for these pairs of numbers, what rules do you find?

Given two integers:
- if one is a factor of the other, it is the highest common factor of both of them
- if they are relatively prime, their highest common factor is 1.

✏ Practice 1.5

1. Write the correct numbers in the diagram below.

factors of 24   factors of 36

common factors of 24 and 36

The highest common factor of 24 and 36 is _____.

2. Which pairs of numbers are relatively prime?

3 and 5   6 and 9   14 and 15   18 and 1

3. Find the highest common factor of the numbers in each pair.

12 and 8   13 and 7   11 and 44   45 and 60

1.6 Common multiples and lowest common multiple

Think!

At a city's central railway station, line 1 trains depart every three minutes and line 3 trains depart every 4 minutes. The first trains on both lines depart at the same time in the morning, at 6 a.m. How long will it be before trains on both lines depart at the same time again?

After 6 a.m., departure times of line 1 trains are multiples of 3 minutes, and departure times of line 3 trains are multiples of 4 minutes. The question can be answered by working out the lowest common multiple of 3 and 4.

The multiples of 3 are 3, 6, 12, 15, 18, 21, 24, 27…

The multiples of 4 are 4, 8, 12, 16, 20, 24, 28, 32, 36, 40…

The common multiples of 3 and 4 are 12, 24… and the lowest one is 12.

multiples of 3

3 6 9	12	4 8 16
15 18 21	24	20 28 32
27 …	…	…

multiples of 4

common multiples of 3 and 4

So, trains on line 1 and line 3 will depart at the same time again after 12 minutes.

> Multiples that are common to two or more numbers are called **common multiples** and the smallest one is called their **lowest common multiple**.

Example 1 Work out the lowest common multiple of 18 and 30.

Solution

Method 1:   The multiples of 18 are 18, 36, 54, 72, 90…

The multiples of 30 are 30, 60, 90, 120, 150…

So, the lowest common multiple of 18 and 30 is 90.

Is there a more efficient way?

Method 2:   Use prime factorisation.

$$18 = 2 \times 3 \times 3$$
$$30 = 2 \times 3 \times 5$$

The common factors of 18 and 30 should include all the prime factors of 18 and 30. You need to choose all the prime factors that are common to both numbers, then all the prime factors that appear in only one of the numbers.

So here you choose one 2 and one 3, and then the extra 3 from 18 and the 5 from 30.

Multiplying these numbers $2 \times 3 \times 3 \times 5$ gives the product 90 as the lowest common multiple of 18 and 30.

prime factors of 18   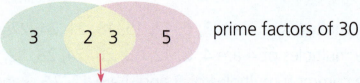   prime factors of 30

common prime factors of 18 and 30

> To work out the lowest common multiple of two integers, first pick out all their common prime factors and then pick out the 'extra' prime factors of all the numbers. Multiply all these prime factors together, then the product is the lowest common multiple of the integers.

Method 3:   To be more efficient, you can also use short division.

$$\begin{array}{r|rr} 2 & 18 & 30 \\ \hline 3 & 9 & 15 \\ \hline & 3 & 5 \end{array}$$

Divide by the common prime factor 2.
Divide by the common prime factor 3.
Continue until the two quotients are relatively prime.

2 and 3 are the common prime factors. 3 and 5 are the remaining prime factors that have been picked out, but are not common prime factors.

The lowest common multiple of 18 and 30 is 2 × 3 × 3 × 5 = 90.

Example 2 Work out the lowest common multiple of 36 and 84.

Solution

$$\begin{array}{r|rr} 2 & 36 & 84 \\ \hline 2 & 18 & 42 \\ \hline 3 & 9 & 21 \\ \hline & 3 & 7 \end{array}$$

Divide by the common prime factor 2.
Divide by the common prime factor 2 again.
Divide by the common prime factor 3.
Continue until the two quotients are relatively prime.

The lowest common multiple of 36 and 84 is 2 × 2 × 3 × 3 × 7 = 252.

Example 3 Work out the highest common factor and the lowest common multiple of 30 and 45.

Solution

$$\begin{array}{r|rr} 3 & 30 & 45 \\ \hline 5 & 10 & 15 \\ \hline & 2 & 3 \end{array}$$

Divide by the common prime factor 3.
Divide by the common prime factor 5.
Continue until the two quotients are relatively prime.

The highest common factor of 30 and 45 is 3 × 5 = 15.
The lowest common multiple of 30 and 45 is 3 × 5 × 2 × 3 = 90.

a. The lowest common multiple of 3 and 15 is _____ .

b. The lowest common multiple of 18 and 36 is _____ .

c. The lowest common multiple of 8 and 9 is _____ .

d. The lowest common multiple of 8 and 15 is _____ .

In finding the lowest common multiple for these pairs of numbers, what rules do you find?

> Given two integers:
> * if one of the two integers is a multiple of the other integer, it is their lowest common multiple
> * if the two integers are relatively prime, their product is their lowest common multiple.

Practice 1.6

1. If $A = 2 \times 2 \times 3 \times 5 \times 7$ and $B = 2 \times 3 \times 3 \times 5 \times 5$, the lowest common multiple of A and B is _____, and their highest common factor is _____ .

2.

The product of two integers must be their lowest common multiple.

A common multiple of two integers must be divisible exactly by the two integers.

Are Dylan and Emma correct? Why?

3. Find the lowest common multiple of the numbers in each pair.

7 and 21   8 and 12   9 and 45   18 and 48

Unit summary

You have already learned about division of two numbers in earlier work. You know that division may have one of two different results – working out exactly or having a remainder. Division in which the quotient is an integer without a remainder is called **exact division**.

For exact division, you can apply concepts such as common factors, highest common factors, lowest common multiple and methods of prime factorisation. What you have learned in this unit lays the foundation for learning operations with fractions in the near future.

The framework of this unit is shown below.

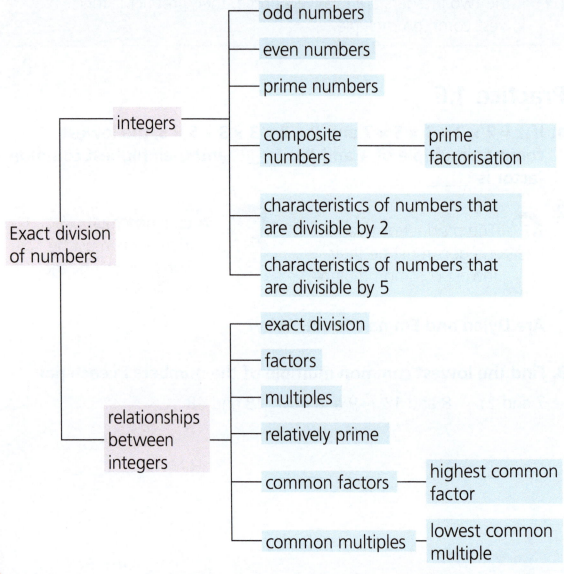

Extension activity: Finding the lowest common multiple of three integers

 Think!

How can you find the lowest common multiple of three integers?

Calculate the lowest common multiple of 8, 12 and 30.

Start by decomposing 8, 12 and 30 into prime factors.

$$8 = 2 \times 2 \times 2$$
$$12 = 2 \times 2 \times 3$$
$$30 = 2 \times \quad 3 \times 5$$

The lowest common multiple of 8, 12 and 30 should contain not just all the prime factors of 8 but also of 12 and 30. However, remember that you only pick up each common factor once.

So the lowest common multiple of 8, 12 and 30 is the product of the prime factors that are common to all three numbers (just one number, 2), then all the 'extra' prime factors in the other numbers (one 2 from 8 and 12 and one 3 from 12 and 30) and the remaining prime factors (one 2 from 8 and one 5 from 30).

So, you can conclude that the lowest common multiple of 8, 12 and 30 is

$2 \times 2 \times 2 \times 3 \times 5 = 120$.

To calculate more efficiently, you can use short division.

2	8	12	30	Divide all three numbers by the common factor 2.
2	4	6	15	Divide 4 and 6 by the common factor 2 again.
3	2	3	15	Divide 3 and 15 by the common factor 3.
	2	1	5	Continue dividing until all the quotients are relatively prime.

The lowest common multiple of 8, 12 and 30 is $2 \times 2 \times 2 \times 3 \times 5 = 120$.

Example   Calculate the lowest common multiple of 10, 12 and 15.

Solution

5	10	12	15	Divide 10 and 15 by the common factor 5.
2	2	12	3	Divide 2 and 12 by the common factor 2.
3	1	6	3	Divide 6 and 3 by the common factor 3.
	1	2	1	Continue dividing until all the quotients are relatively prime.

The lowest common multiple of 10, 12 and 15 is $2 \times 2 \times 3 \times 5 = 60$.

Think!

1. What is the difference between finding the lowest common multiple of two integers and of three integers?

2. There are about 350 oranges in a basket. You can keep taking out 3, 4 or 5 oranges to empty the basket, with none left over. How many oranges are there in the basket?

Extra reading material: Producing a table of prime numbers

Do you know how to make a list of all the prime numbers between 1 and 100?

You use a sieve! Here is the method:

- List all the integers from 1 to 100.
- Cross out number 1.
- Circle all the prime numbers less than 10.
- Cross out all the multiples of 2.
- Cross out all the multiples of 3.
- Cross out all the multiples of 5.
- Cross out all the multiples of 7.

1	2	3	4	5	6	7	8	9	10
11	12	13	14	15	16	17	18	19	20
21	22	23	24	25	26	27	28	29	30
31	32	33	34	35	36	37	38	39	40
41	42	43	44	45	46	47	48	49	50
51	52	53	54	55	56	57	58	59	60
61	62	63	64	65	66	67	68	69	70
71	72	73	74	75	76	77	78	79	80
81	82	83	84	85	86	87	88	89	90
91	92	93	94	95	96	97	98	99	100

- Write the numbers that are left in order. Then you have a list of prime numbers up to 100.

Think!

Why don't we continue crossing out numbers after the multiples of 7?

About 2000 years ago, Eratosthenes, a Greek mathematician, the chief librarian at the Library of Alexandria, used this method to find all the prime numbers from 1 to 1000. Just like sieving stones from sand, he sieved the prime numbers from the positive integers. It was called the **sieve of Eratosthenes**. Nowadays this is the main method for finding prime numbers.

Mathematicians often use prime numbers from 1 to 100. After the four prime numbers 2, 3, 5 and 7, other prime numbers are two-digit odd numbers, and their ones digit is always 1, 3, 7 or 9.

So, how can we represent prime numbers? One mathematician found these rules.

$$1 \times 1 + 1 + 41 = 43 \qquad 2 \times 2 + 2 + 41 = 47$$
$$3 \times 3 + 3 + 41 = 53 \qquad 4 \times 4 + 4 + 41 = 61$$

The numbers 43, 47, 53 and 61 are all prime numbers. So the mathematician thought that he had found the formula to construct prime numbers. What a wonderful invention that was! He was so excited. When he calculated $39 \times 39 + 39 + 41 = 1601$, he found that 1601 is still a prime number. However, when he continued his calculations, he found that $40 \times 40 + 40 + 41 = 1681 = 41 \times 41$. 1681 is a composite number, not a prime number.

This raised the question of whether the number of prime numbers is finite. If it is finite, we can use a sieve to list all the prime numbers. However, about 2300 years ago, Euclid, a Greek mathematician, had already proved that the number of prime numbers is infinite. So far, mathematicians haven't found an effective formula to construct prime numbers or to produce prime numbers. So if we want to find a large prime number, we have to use a calculator. Research on finding large prime numbers is still continuing.

Investigation activity: Using prime factors to find factors

If we want to write the factors of an integer, we can try dividing it by prime numbers, one by one, which will produce factor pairs, and eventually work out the total number of factors. For example, how many factors does the number 180 have? We can write all the factors, then count them. Then we will know the answer.

The factors of 180 are 1, 180; 2, 90; 3, 60; 4, 45; 5, 36; 6, 30; 9, 20; 10, 18; 12, 15.

There are 9 pairs and 18 numbers in all.

For large composite numbers, finding factors in this way not only wastes time but also makes it easy to miss some.

Is there another, better way? Let's explore the relationship between the number of factors and the number of prime factors.

Use prime factorisation of the numbers 4, 27 and 16. Write all the factors.

	Prime factorisation	All the factors	The number of factors
4	$4 = 2 \times 2$		
27	$27 = 3 \times 3 \times 3$		
16	$16 = 2 \times 2 \times 2 \times 2$		

Can you find the relationship between the number of factors and the number of prime factors of these numbers? Complete the table.

	Prime factorisation	All the factors	The number of factors
6	$6 = 2 \times 3$		
12	$12 = 2 \times 2 \times 3$		
18	$18 = 2 \times 3 \times 3$		

Can you find the relationship between the number of factors and the number of prime factors of these numbers?

Now try to solve these problems!

1. $210 = 21 \times 10 = 2 \times 3 \times 5 \times 7$

Can you find the factors of 210 quickly and write them all down?

2. Write all the factors of the number 1260.

Is your research correct? Use the internet to find the information you need.

Unit Two
Fractions

Do you know the height and mass of the famous basketball players Yao Ming and Bateer?

My height is $\frac{3}{5}$ of Yao Ming's and my mass is $\frac{7}{20}$ of his.

My height is $\frac{5}{7}$ of Bateer's and my mass is $\frac{9}{26}$ of his.

Yao Ming's height is 226 centimetres and his mass is 134 kilograms.

Bateer's height is 210 centimetres and his mass is 130 kilograms.

Who is taller, Dylan or Emma? And who is heavier?
When you have learned the mathematics in this unit, you will be able to solve the problem for yourself.

Section One: The meaning and properties of fractions

2.1 Fractions and division

When we divide a whole into several equal parts, one or some parts can be represented by a fraction.

For example, think about a whole cake divided into 8 equal pieces. One piece of the cake is represented as $\frac{1}{8}$.

Then three pupils, Emma, Dylan and Poppy, each eat one of the 8 pieces. This means these three pupils together eat $\frac{3}{8}$ of the whole cake.

This still leaves 5 pieces, which is $\frac{5}{8}$ of the original cake.

Now think about 16 cakes, all the same size. We can think of them as a whole. If we think of two of the cakes as one part, we can divide the whole into 8 parts. Each part is $\frac{1}{8}$ of the 16 cakes.

Observation

Look at picture **A**. If an orange is shared equally by 4 people, the orange is divided into 4 equal pieces. By the rules of division, this is $1 \div 4$. Each person can have one piece of the orange.

We can write $\frac{1}{4}$ to represent one piece (picture **B**).

picture **A**

picture **B**

Suppose two oranges of the same size are shared equally among 4 people. We can use division to represent it as 2 ÷ 4 (picture **C**). When one orange is shared equally among 4 people everyone gets $\frac{1}{4}$ of the orange. When two oranges of the same size are shared equally among 4 people, everyone gets $\frac{1}{4}$ of the two oranges (picture **D**). So everyone can get two $\frac{1}{4}$s. This is the same as $\frac{2}{4}$ of one orange (picture **E**).

picture **C**

picture **D**

picture **E**

We can think of $\frac{1}{4}$ as being equivalent to 1 ÷ 4, and $\frac{2}{4}$ as being equivalent to 2 ÷ 4. So we can conclude that $1 \div 4 = \frac{1}{4}$, and $2 \div 4 = \frac{2}{4}$.

Summary

$$\text{dividend} \div \text{divisor} = \frac{\text{dividend}}{\text{divisor}}$$

Think about two integers, p and q. We can write the fraction $\frac{p}{q}$ to represent $p \div q$. So $p \div q = \frac{p}{q}$, where p is the **numerator** and q is the **denominator**.

$$3 \div 1 = \frac{3}{1} = 3$$
$$5 \div 1 = \frac{5}{1} = 5$$

$\frac{p}{q}$ is read as **p out of q**.
Note that, when $q = 1$, $\frac{p}{q} = p$.

Think!

1. Is $\frac{1}{4}$ of an orange equal to $\frac{1}{4}$ of two oranges? Why?

2. Can a fraction correspond to a point on the number line?

Look at the picture. Divide the length between adjacent integers (0 and 1, and 1 and 2) on the number line into 5 equal parts and mark them. Starting from 0, from left to right, the third point and the seventh point respectively represent the fractions $\frac{3}{5}$ and $\frac{7}{5}$.

How can you use points on the number line to represent fractions $\frac{2}{7}$ and $\frac{9}{7}$?

0     $\frac{3}{5}$ 1 $\frac{7}{5}$ 2

Practice 2.1

1. Each pattern represents a whole, and can be taken as 1. Write the fraction represented by the shaded region in each pattern.

   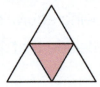

2. Look at this array of cars. What fraction can be used to represent the red cars out of all the cars?

3. Use fractions to represent these division sentences.

a. $3 \div 2$ **b.** $2 \div 9$ **c.** $7 \div 8$

d. $5 \div 12$ **e.** $31 \div 5$ **f.** $8 \div 2$

4. Write each fraction as a division sentence.

a. $\dfrac{4}{3}$ b. $\dfrac{5}{4}$ c. $\dfrac{4}{2}$ d. $\dfrac{1}{3}$ e. $\dfrac{13}{22}$ f. $\dfrac{3}{10}$

5. Write the fractions represented by points A, B and C on the number line.

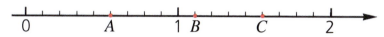

2.2 Basic properties of fractions

Observation

Dylan, Emma and Poppy are colouring sheets of paper. $\dfrac{3}{4}$ of each sheet is coloured.

They fold the paper into different patterns to show equal divisions.

Look at their sheets of paper. What conclusion can you make?

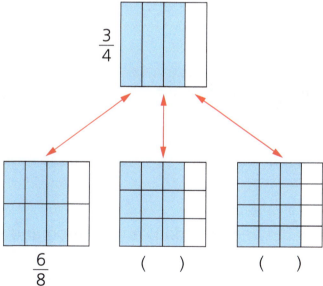

Although all the sheets of paper are the same size they have been folded to make different equal divisions.

What fractions can be written to represent the coloured region of the paper? What is the relationship between these fractions?

These fractions are equivalent: $\dfrac{3}{4} = \dfrac{6}{8} = \dfrac{9}{12} = \dfrac{12}{16}$

Multiplying the numerator and the denominator of $\frac{3}{4}$ by 2, 3 and 4 respectively gives $\frac{6}{8}$, $\frac{9}{12}$ and $\frac{12}{16}$.

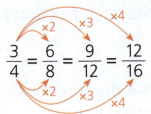

$$\frac{3}{4} = \frac{6}{8} = \frac{9}{12} = \frac{12}{16}$$

Dividing the numerator and the denominator of $\frac{12}{16}$, $\frac{9}{12}$ and $\frac{6}{8}$ by 4, 3 and 2 respectively gives $\frac{3}{4}$.

$$\frac{12}{16} = \frac{9}{12} = \frac{6}{8} = \frac{3}{4}$$

Think!

1. **Use the fractions to describe the coloured region of each shape. What is the relationship between these fractions?**

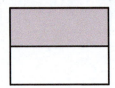 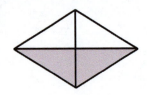 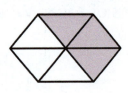 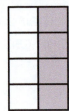

2. **Fill in the brackets: $\frac{3}{5} = \frac{(\quad)}{20}$.**

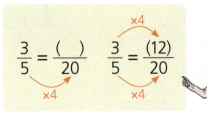

$$\frac{3}{5} = \frac{(\quad)}{20} \qquad \frac{3}{5} = \frac{(12)}{20}$$

Summary

From the relationship between fractions and division and the basic property of division, you know:

> **The basic property of fractions**
>
> Multiplying or dividing both the numerator and the denominator by a number that is not 0 ($\neq 0$) gives a new fraction that is equivalent to the original one.
>
> $$\frac{a}{b} = \frac{a \times k}{b \times k} = \frac{a \div n}{b \div n} \qquad (b \neq 0, k \neq 0, n \neq 0)$$

Example 1 List three fractions that are equivalent to $\frac{2}{5}$.

Are there only three fractions that are equivalent to $\frac{2}{5}$?

Solution $\frac{2 \times 2}{5 \times 2} = \frac{4}{10}$ so you know that $\frac{4}{10} = \frac{2}{5}$ from the basic property of fractions.

In the same way, you know that $\frac{6}{15} = \frac{2}{5}$, and $\frac{10}{25} = \frac{2}{5}$.

So $\frac{4}{10}$, $\frac{6}{15}$ and $\frac{10}{25}$ are three fractions that are equivalent to $\frac{2}{5}$.

There are many fractions like this. Can you list any others?

Example 2 Convert $\frac{2}{5}$ and $\frac{8}{60}$ into equivalent fractions with a denominator of 15.

Solution $\frac{2}{5} = \frac{2 \times 3}{5 \times 3} = \frac{6}{15}$, $\frac{8}{60} = \frac{8 \div 4}{60 \div 4} = \frac{2}{15}$

Using the basic property of fractions, you can convert a fraction into another fraction that is equal to the original one but with a different denominator from the original one.

Practice 2.2 (1)

1. Fill in the brackets to make the equation true.

a. $\dfrac{9}{15} = \dfrac{3 \times (\quad)}{5 \times (\quad)}$

b. $\dfrac{2 \times (\quad)}{9 \times (\quad)} = \dfrac{8}{(\quad)}$

c. $\dfrac{5 \times (\quad)}{2 \times (\quad)} = \dfrac{(\quad)}{14}$

d. $\dfrac{5 \div (\quad)}{20 \div (\quad)} = \dfrac{(\quad)}{4}$

2. Write three equivalent fractions with different denominators for each of these fractions.

a. $\frac{1}{4}$ b. $\frac{5}{7}$ c. $\frac{4}{6}$ d. $\frac{10}{4}$

3. Draw points on a number line to represent these numbers: $\frac{1}{2}$, $\frac{2}{4}$ and $\frac{4}{8}$. What conclusion can you make?

4. Convert $\frac{2}{3}$ and $\frac{8}{30}$ into equivalent fractions with a denominator of 15.

5. Fill in the brackets.

   a. $\frac{1}{4} = \frac{(\quad)}{12}$ b. $\frac{3}{7} = \frac{(\quad)}{56}$ c. $\frac{6}{5} = \frac{30}{(\quad)}$

   d. $\frac{(\quad)}{10} = \frac{4}{20}$ e. $\frac{36}{24} = \frac{(\quad)}{8}$ f. $\frac{7}{35} = \frac{1}{(\quad)}$

   g. $\frac{18}{(\quad)} = \frac{6}{12}$ h. $\frac{20}{16} = \frac{5}{(\quad)}$

Think!

| What is the highest common factor of 12 and 30? | → | Can you write three fractions that are equivalent to $\frac{12}{30}$ with denominators that are smaller than 30? |

The common factors of 12 and 30 that are greater than 1 are 2, 3 and 6. Using the basic property of fractions:

$$\frac{12}{30} = \frac{12 \div 2}{30 \div 2} = \frac{6}{15}, \quad \frac{12}{30} = \frac{12 \div 3}{30 \div 3} = \frac{4}{10}, \quad \frac{12}{30} = \frac{12 \div 6}{30 \div 6} = \frac{2}{5}$$

| Can you find any other fractions equivalent to $\frac{12}{30}$ with denominators smaller than 30? | → | So, the three fractions that are equivalent to $\frac{12}{30}$ with denominators that are smaller than 30 are $\frac{6}{15}$, $\frac{4}{10}$ and $\frac{2}{5}$. |

Of $\frac{6}{15}$, $\frac{4}{10}$ and $\frac{2}{5}$, only in $\frac{2}{5}$ are the numerator and the denominator relatively prime.

Such a fraction is in its **simplest form**.

You have **reduced** the fraction to its **lowest terms**.

> A fraction in which the numerator and denominator are relatively prime is written in its simplest form.

The method for converting $\frac{12}{30}$ into $\frac{6}{15}$, $\frac{4}{10}$ and $\frac{2}{5}$, which are equivalent to $\frac{12}{30}$, is called **cancelling**.

Dividing the numerator and the denominator of a fraction by their common factors is called cancelling.

You can simplify fractions by cancelling.

Example 3 Cancel $\frac{12}{18}$ and write it as a fraction in its lowest terms.

Does cancelling turn $\frac{12}{30}$ into $\frac{24}{60}$?

Solution $\frac{12}{18} = \frac{2 \times 2 \times 3}{2 \times 3 \times 3} = \frac{2}{3}$

You can also write this as:

You can also just divide 12 and 18 by 6.

$$\frac{\overset{\overset{2}{\cancel{6}}}{\cancel{12}}}{\underset{\underset{3}{\cancel{9}}}{\cancel{18}}} = \frac{2}{3}$$

First, divide 12 and 18 by the common factor 2 to get 6 and 9. Then, divide 6 and 9 by the common factor 3 to get 2 and 3.

To reduce the fraction to its lowest terms, you can divide the numerator and the denominator by their highest common factor. You can also cancel repeatedly until the numerator and the denominator are relatively prime.

Example 4 **a.** What fraction is 24 cm of 1 m?

b. Emma spends 9 hours sleeping every day. What fraction of 24 hours (a day) is 9 hours?

Give each fraction in its simplest form.

Solution **a.** 1 m = 100 cm

$$24 \div 100 = \frac{24}{100} = \frac{4 \times 6}{4 \times 25} = \frac{6}{25}$$

Note: when writing fractions that involve measurements, it is important to use the same units in the numerator and denominator.

24 cm is $\frac{6}{25}$ of 1 m.

b. $9 \div 24 = \frac{9}{24} = \frac{3}{8}$

The time Emma spends sleeping is $\frac{3}{8}$ of 24 hours (a day).

Practice 2.2 (2)

1. Write the highest common factor for each pair of numbers.

    a. 24, 12   **b.** 9, 24   **c.** 20, 45

2. Find the fractions that are in their simplest form. Cancel the rest into their lowest terms.

$$\frac{2}{10}, \frac{12}{13}, \frac{3}{7}, \frac{21}{33}, \frac{2}{81}, \frac{22}{35}, \frac{15}{4}, \frac{24}{15}$$

3. Rewrite the fractions in their simplest form.

$$\frac{20}{70}, \frac{15}{35}, \frac{42}{45}, \frac{21}{36}, \frac{33}{55}, \frac{26}{52}, \frac{50}{120}, \frac{28}{35}, \frac{81}{18}$$

4. What is 15 minutes as a fraction of 1 hour?

5. There are 46 pupils in Year 6 Class 1, and 28 of them are girls. What fraction of the whole class are girls?

6. Is Emma's explanation right or wrong? Give an example to explain.

> If one of the numerator and the denominator of a fraction is an odd number and the other is an even number, the fraction must be in its lowest terms.

Example 5 The graph shows the masses of all the boys in Year 6 Class 2. Look carefully at the graph, then answer these questions.

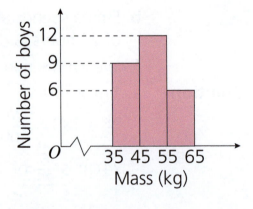

    a. What fraction of the boys weigh 35–45 kg (including 35 kg but not 45 kg)?

    b. What fraction of the boys weigh 55–65 kg (including 55 kg but not 65 kg)?

Solution The total number of boys is 12 + 9 + 6 = 27.

There are 9 boys who weigh 35–45 kg (including 35 kg but not 45 kg). There are 6 boys who weigh 55–65 kg (including 55 kg but not 65 kg).

a. $9 \div 27 = \dfrac{9}{27} = \dfrac{1}{3}$

$\dfrac{1}{3}$ of the boys weigh 35–45 kg (including 35 kg but not 45 kg).

b. $6 \div 27 = \dfrac{6}{27} = \dfrac{2}{9}$

$\dfrac{2}{9}$ of the boys weigh 55–65 kg (including 55 kg but not 65 kg).

Example 6 The table shows how much electricity Emma's family consumed in the second half of last year.

Month	Jul	Aug	Sep	Oct	Nov	Dec
Electricity consumption (kWh)	95	77	80	205	217	136

a. What was the highest amount of electricity consumed in the fourth quarter (October to December)? What fraction is this of the electricity consumed in this quarter?

b. What fraction of the consumption in the whole of the second half of the year was the electricity consumption in the fourth quarter?

Solution

a. Emma's family consumed the most electricity in November.

The total electricity consumption in the fourth quarter is 205 + 217 + 136 = 558 (kWh).

$217 \div 558 = \dfrac{217}{558} = \dfrac{7}{18}$

The electricity consumption in November is $\dfrac{7}{18}$ of the total electricity consumption in the fourth quarter.

b. The total electricity consumption in the second half of the year is 558 + 95 + 77 + 80 = 810 (kWh).

$558 \div 810 = \dfrac{518}{810} = \dfrac{31}{45}$

The total electricity consumption in the fourth quarter is $\dfrac{31}{45}$ of the total electricity consumption in the second half of the year.

✏ Practice 2.2 (3)

1. There are 50 000 books in a public library. Among them, there are 20 000 reference books, 18 000 novels, 10 000 popular science books and 2000 other books. What fraction of all the books is each kind of book?

2. Each of the 46 pupils in Year 6 Class 3 chose their favourite hobby. The graph shows how many pupils chose the hobbies listed. Some pupils had no hobbies.

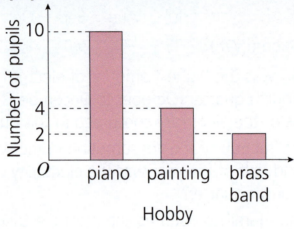

   a. What fraction of the whole class enjoy painting?
   b. If you take piano or brass band as one group who have musical hobbies, what fraction of the whole class have musical hobbies?
   c. What fraction of the pupils who have hobbies have musical hobbies?

3. Investigate the birth months of the pupils in your class, then complete the table.

Month	1	2	3	4	5	6	7	8	9	10	11	12
Number of pupils												
What fraction of the whole class have birthdays in this month?												

2.3 Comparing fractions

You learned how to compare two fractions in an earlier year. Do you remember how to do it?

To compare two fractions with the same denominator, such as $\frac{2}{9}$ and $\frac{5}{9}$, you only need to compare their numerators. If the numerator is larger, the fraction is larger.

So $\frac{2}{9} < \frac{5}{9}$.

You can mark $\frac{2}{9}$ and $\frac{5}{9}$ on a number line. From the diagram you can see that the dot that represents $\frac{2}{9}$ is to the left of the dot that represents $\frac{5}{9}$.

Comparing two fractions is clear on the number line. The number represented by the dot on the left is smaller than the number represented by the dot on the right.

Can a cable of diameter $\frac{5}{6}$ cm fit inside a pipe of internal diameter $\frac{7}{8}$ cm?

We just need to compare $\frac{5}{6}$ and $\frac{7}{8}$.

But $\frac{5}{6}$ and $\frac{7}{8}$ have different denominators. How can we compare them?

Can we turn them into fractions with the same denominator to deal with the problem?

The denominators of $\frac{5}{6}$ and $\frac{7}{8}$ are 6 and 8.

We need to convert the two fractions so that they both have the same denominator, so the denominator must be a common multiple of 6 and 8. The denominator is called a **common denominator**. There are countless common multiples of 6 and 8. We usually take the lowest common multiple. The lowest common multiple of 6 and 8 is 24, so take 24 as the common multiple, and then turn $\frac{5}{6}$ and $\frac{7}{8}$ into fractions with denominator 24.

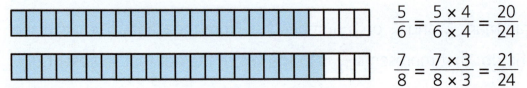

$$\frac{5}{6} = \frac{5 \times 4}{6 \times 4} = \frac{20}{24}$$

$$\frac{7}{8} = \frac{7 \times 3}{8 \times 3} = \frac{21}{24}$$

$$\frac{20}{24} < \frac{21}{24} \quad \text{so} \quad \frac{5}{6} < \frac{7}{8}$$

We can also compare $\frac{5}{6}$ and $\frac{7}{8}$ on a number line.

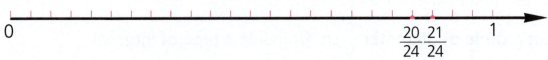

So a cable of diameter $\frac{5}{6}$ cm can fit inside a pipe of internal diameter $\frac{7}{8}$ cm.

> To compare fractions, we first convert them to equivalent fractions with a common denominator, which is the lowest common multiple of the original denominators. This denominator is called the **lowest common denominator**, or **LCD**.

Example 1 Convert the two fractions in each pair into equivalent fractions with the same denominator and compare them.

      a. $\frac{2}{5}$ and $\frac{3}{7}$ **b.** $\frac{9}{25}$ and $\frac{4}{15}$

Solution   **a.** Use the lowest common multiple of 5 and 7, which is 35, as the common denominator.

$$\frac{2}{5} = \frac{2 \times 7}{5 \times 7} = \frac{14}{35}, \frac{3}{7} = \frac{3 \times 5}{7 \times 5} = \frac{15}{35}$$

$$\frac{14}{35} < \frac{15}{35}, \text{ so } \frac{2}{5} < \frac{3}{7}$$

b. Use the lowest common multiple of 15 and 25, which is 75, as the common denominator.

$$\frac{9}{25} = \frac{9 \times 3}{25 \times 3} = \frac{27}{75}, \frac{4}{15} = \frac{4 \times 5}{15 \times 5} = \frac{20}{75}$$

$$\frac{27}{75} > \frac{20}{75}, \text{ so } \frac{9}{25} > \frac{4}{15}$$

Example 2 Convert $\frac{1}{3}$, $\frac{3}{4}$ and $\frac{5}{9}$ into fractions with the same denominator and compare them.

Solution Use the lowest common multiple of 3, 4 and 9, which is 36, as the common denominator.

$$\frac{1}{3} = \frac{1 \times 12}{3 \times 12} = \frac{12}{36}, \frac{3}{4} = \frac{3 \times 9}{4 \times 9} = \frac{27}{36}, \frac{5}{9} = \frac{5 \times 4}{9 \times 4} = \frac{20}{36}$$

$$\frac{12}{36} < \frac{20}{36} < \frac{27}{36}, \text{ so } \frac{1}{3} < \frac{5}{9} < \frac{3}{4}$$

Practice 2.3

1. **Convert the two fractions in each pair into equivalent fractions with the same denominator and compare them.**

   a. $\frac{2}{3}$ and $\frac{1}{6}$ **b.** $\frac{2}{5}$ and $\frac{1}{3}$ **c.** $\frac{2}{7}$ and $\frac{2}{3}$

   d. $\frac{5}{4}$ and $\frac{1}{6}$ **e.** $\frac{3}{14}$ and $\frac{5}{16}$ **f.** $\frac{11}{20}$ and $\frac{5}{8}$

2. **Convert $\frac{3}{4}$, $\frac{5}{7}$ and $\frac{7}{9}$ into equivalent fractions with the same denominator and order them from smallest to greatest.**

3. **Is there a fraction, in its simplest form, smaller than $\frac{5}{6}$ but with a denominator of 12?**
   If so, write all the fractions, in their simplest form, that meet these requirements.

Section Two: Operations with fractions

2.4 Addition and subtraction of fractions

 **Think!**

$$\frac{1}{2} + \frac{1}{3} = ?$$

$$\frac{1}{2} + \frac{1}{3} = \frac{2}{5}$$

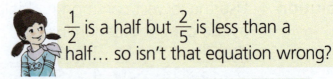

$\frac{1}{2}$ is a half but $\frac{2}{5}$ is less than a half... so isn't that equation wrong?

 Use drawing and observation methods to think about it.

1. In May, Dylan used $\frac{1}{5}$ of his pocket money to buy magazines and $\frac{2}{5}$ of his pocket money to buy the materials to make model aeroplanes. What fraction of his pocket money did Dylan spend on magazines and materials for model aeroplanes altogether in May?

It's just a question of adding two fractions with the same denominator, which is $\frac{1}{5} + \frac{2}{5}$.

Do you remember how to add and subtract fractions with the same denominator from what you learned in earlier years?

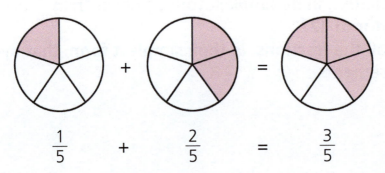

$$\frac{1}{5} \qquad + \qquad \frac{2}{5} \qquad = \qquad \frac{3}{5}$$

To add fractions with the same denominator, keep the denominator the same and add the two numerators.

So Dylan spent $\frac{3}{5}$ of his pocket money on magazines and materials for model aeroplanes in May.

2. In June, Dylan used $\frac{1}{4}$ of his pocket money to buy magazines, and $\frac{2}{3}$ of his pocket money to buy materials to make models. What fraction of his pocket money did Dylan spend on magazines and materials for models altogether in June?

Again, you need to add two fractions, but $\frac{1}{4}$ and $\frac{2}{3}$ have different denominators. How can you add the two fractions?

You can use the method that you have learned before to convert the two fractions into equivalent fractions with the same denominator.

$$\frac{1}{4} + \frac{2}{3}$$
$$= \frac{3}{12} + \frac{8}{12} = \frac{3+8}{12} = \frac{11}{12}$$

How can we change the two fractions so that they have the same denominator? This is reduction of fractions to a common denominator.

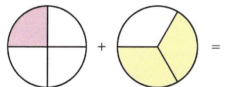

So Dylan spent $\frac{11}{12}$ of his pocket money on magazines and materials for models in June.

3. In June, Dylan used $\frac{2}{3}$ of his pocket money to buy materials for his model aeroplanes and model ships.

If $\frac{5}{12}$ of Dylan's pocket money was spent on materials for model aeroplanes, what fraction was spent on materials for model ships?

This is a subtraction of two fractions with different denominators.

$$\frac{2}{3} - \frac{5}{12} = \frac{8}{12} - \frac{5}{12} \qquad = \qquad \frac{8-5}{12} \qquad = \qquad \frac{3}{12} = \frac{1}{4}$$

reduction of fractions to a common denominator

cancelling

So Dylan spent $\frac{1}{4}$ of his pocket money on materials to build model aeroplanes in June.

Summary

To add or subtract fractions with different denominators, first reduce the fractions to a common denominator. Then use the method for addition and subtraction of fractions with the same denominator.

Example 1 Calculate.

a. $\dfrac{3}{8} + \dfrac{7}{12}$ **b.** $\dfrac{5}{6} - \dfrac{1}{3}$ **c.** $\dfrac{2}{3} + \dfrac{1}{4} - \dfrac{1}{5}$

Solution

a. $\dfrac{3}{8} + \dfrac{7}{12} = \dfrac{9}{24} + \dfrac{14}{24} = \dfrac{23}{24}$

b. $\dfrac{5}{6} - \dfrac{1}{3} = \dfrac{5}{6} - \dfrac{2}{6} = \dfrac{3}{6} = \dfrac{1}{2}$

c. $\dfrac{2}{3} + \dfrac{1}{4} - \dfrac{1}{5} = \dfrac{40}{60} + \dfrac{15}{60} - \dfrac{12}{60}$

$\qquad = \dfrac{40 + 15 - 12}{60} = \dfrac{43}{60}$

The lowest common multiple of 3, 4 and 5 is 60.

The method for mixed operations in addition and subtraction of fractions is the same as for mixed operations of addition and subtraction of integers.

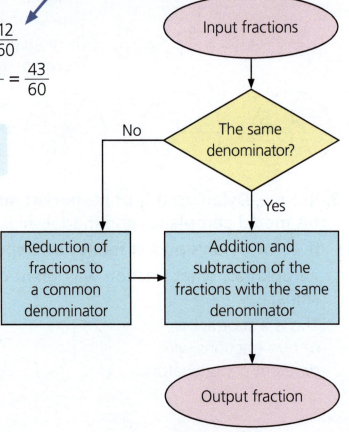

Generally, you should cancel the fraction in your answer to its lowest terms.

The flowchart shows the method for addition and subtraction of fractions.

Practice 2.4 (1)

1. Calculate.

  a. $\dfrac{3}{4} + \dfrac{5}{8}$ **b.** $\dfrac{2}{7} + \dfrac{3}{5}$ **c.** $\dfrac{4}{5} - \dfrac{3}{10}$

  d. $\dfrac{11}{12} - \dfrac{3}{4} + \dfrac{1}{6}$ **e.** $\dfrac{12}{25} + \dfrac{1}{4}$ **f.** $\dfrac{3}{4} + \dfrac{5}{12} - \dfrac{5}{6}$

2. The school bought a tonne of sand to repair the sports pavilion and to fill the sandpits used for high jump and long jump. $\dfrac{4}{5}$ of the sand was used on repairing the pavilion and $\dfrac{1}{8}$ of the sand was used to fill the sandpits. How much sand was used in total? How much sand was left?

3. During his three-week winter holiday, Dylan finished $\dfrac{1}{5}$ of his homework in the first week and $\dfrac{5}{12}$ of it in the second week. In which week did he finish more homework? How much more? How much homework had Dylan finished in those two weeks?

4. Fill in the missing outputs.

a.

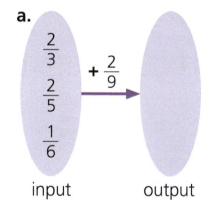

input   output

b.

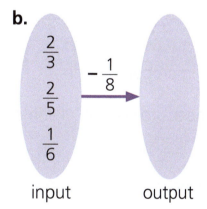

input   output

 Think!

Emma is hiking as part of her fitness training. There is a sign showing 0 km at the start of the hiking trail, then there is a sign every quarter of a kilometre. Emma has reached the seventh sign. How many kilometres has she walked? If the hiking trail is 4 kilometres long, how many kilometres does Emma still have to walk?

Writing the fractions on a number line shows that seven-quarters is equal to one and three-quarters.

$1 + \frac{3}{4}$ is written as $1\frac{3}{4}$ and it means that $\frac{7}{4} = 1\frac{3}{4}$, which is read as one and three-quarters.

So Emma has walked $1\frac{3}{4}$ kilometres.

> A fraction in which the numerator is smaller than the denominator is called a **proper fraction**, while a fraction with the numerator greater than or equal to the denominator is called an **improper fraction**.
>
> A number made up of a positive integer added to a proper fraction is called a **mixed number**.

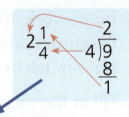

$$4 - \frac{7}{4} = \frac{4}{1} - \frac{7}{4} = \frac{16}{4} - \frac{7}{4} = \frac{9}{4} \qquad \frac{9}{4} = \frac{8}{4} + \frac{1}{4} = 2 + \frac{1}{4} = 2\frac{1}{4}$$

                   improper fraction   proper fraction   mixed number

So Emma still needs to walk $2\frac{1}{4}$ kilometres.

 Think about the relationship between proper fractions, improper fractions and the number 1.

Example 2
Convert these mixed numbers into improper fractions.

a. $3\frac{2}{5}$ **b.** $5\frac{5}{6}$

Solution

a. $3\frac{2}{5} = 3 + \frac{2}{5} = \frac{15}{5} + \frac{2}{5} = \frac{17}{5}$

b. $5\frac{5}{6} = 5 + \frac{5}{6} = \frac{30}{6} + \frac{5}{6} = \frac{35}{6}$

Work it out like this:

$3\frac{2}{5} = \frac{3 \times 5 + 2}{5} = \frac{17}{5}$

Example 3 Convert these improper fractions into mixed numbers and mark them on the number line.

a. $\dfrac{8}{3}$ b. $\dfrac{35}{8}$

Solution a. $\dfrac{8}{3} = \dfrac{6}{3} + \dfrac{2}{3} = 2 + \dfrac{2}{3} = 2\dfrac{2}{3}$

b. $\dfrac{35}{8} = \dfrac{32}{8} + \dfrac{3}{8} = 4 + \dfrac{3}{8} = 4\dfrac{3}{8}$

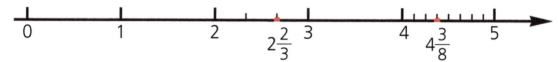

A mixed number is another representation of an improper fraction, but it is easier to estimate the value from the mixed number.

Example 4 Calculate.

a. $\dfrac{5}{3} + \dfrac{3}{5}$ b. $3\dfrac{3}{4} + 1\dfrac{1}{6}$ c. $3\dfrac{5}{12} - \dfrac{11}{4}$

Solution

a. $\dfrac{5}{3} + \dfrac{3}{5} = \dfrac{25}{15} + \dfrac{9}{15} = \dfrac{34}{15} = 2\dfrac{4}{15}$

> Addition of the fractions and integers follows the same mathematical laws: the commutative law and the associative law.

b. $3\dfrac{3}{4} + 1\dfrac{1}{6} = 3 + \dfrac{3}{4} + 1 + \dfrac{1}{6}$

$= (3 + 1) + \dfrac{3}{4} + \dfrac{1}{6}$

$= 4 + \dfrac{9 + 2}{12} = 4\dfrac{11}{12}$

c. $3\dfrac{5}{12} - \dfrac{11}{4} = 3 + \dfrac{5}{12} - \left(2 + \dfrac{3}{4}\right) = 3 - 2 + \dfrac{5}{12} - \dfrac{3}{4}$

$= 1 + \dfrac{5}{12} - \dfrac{3}{4} = \dfrac{12 + 5 - 9}{12} = \dfrac{8}{12} = \dfrac{2}{3}$

> Work it out like this:
>
> $3\dfrac{5}{12} - \dfrac{11}{4} = 3 + \dfrac{5}{12} - \dfrac{11}{4}$
>
> $= \dfrac{36 + 5 - 33}{12} = \dfrac{8}{12} = \dfrac{2}{3}$

Example 5 Calculate: $2\dfrac{2}{3} + \dfrac{2}{7} + 1\dfrac{5}{6}$

Solution

$2\dfrac{2}{3} + \dfrac{2}{7} + 1\dfrac{5}{6} = 2 + \dfrac{2}{3} + \dfrac{2}{7} + 1 + \dfrac{5}{6}$

$= (2 + 1) + \dfrac{2}{3} + \dfrac{5}{6} + \dfrac{2}{7} = 3 + \dfrac{\overset{3}{\cancel{9}}}{\underset{2}{\cancel{6}}} + \dfrac{2}{7} = 3 + \dfrac{25}{14}$

> Don't write the result as $3\dfrac{25}{14}$.

$= 3 + 1 + \dfrac{11}{14} = 4\dfrac{11}{14}$

When adding and subtracting mixed numbers, you can add (or subtract) the integers and the proper fractions separately and then combine the results. Alternatively, you can convert the mixed numbers to improper fractions and then calculate.

If the result of the operation is an improper fraction, then you need to write it as a mixed number.

Example 6

Poppy and Emma took part in a concert. They each sang a song.

Poppy sang for $3\frac{2}{3}$ minutes, while Emma sang for $1\frac{1}{4}$ minutes.

a. How long did they sing altogether?

b. How much longer was Poppy's song than Emma's?

Solution

a. $3\frac{2}{3} + 1\frac{1}{4} = 3 + \frac{2}{3} + 1 + \frac{1}{4} = 4 + \frac{2}{3} + \frac{1}{4} = 4 + \frac{8+3}{12} = 4\frac{11}{12}$ (minutes)

They sang for $4\frac{11}{12}$ minutes altogether.

b. $3\frac{2}{3} - 1\frac{1}{4} = \frac{11}{3} - \frac{5}{4} = \frac{44-15}{12}$

$= \frac{29}{12} = 2\frac{5}{12}$ (minutes) ⬅

$$3\frac{2}{3} - 1\frac{1}{4} = 3 - 1 + \frac{2}{3} - \frac{1}{4}$$
$$= 2 + \frac{8-3}{12}$$
$$= 2\frac{5}{12}$$

Poppy sang for $2\frac{5}{12}$ minutes longer than Emma.

Practice 2.4 (2)

1. Calculate. Give your answers in their simplest form.

    a. $\frac{2}{5} + \frac{11}{10}$ **b.** $\frac{6}{5} - \frac{2}{3}$ **c.** $\frac{5}{3} + \frac{7}{4}$ **d.** $\frac{11}{12} + \frac{4}{3} - \frac{3}{4}$

2. Convert these mixed numbers into improper fractions.

    a. $3\frac{1}{3}$ **b.** $2\frac{3}{4}$ **c.** $7\frac{3}{5}$

    d. $34\frac{1}{2}$ **e.** $9\frac{2}{9}$ **f.** $51\frac{2}{3}$

3. Convert these improper fractions into mixed numbers and mark them on a number line.

    a. $\dfrac{11}{3}$ **b.** $\dfrac{25}{12}$ **c.** $\dfrac{37}{10}$ **d.** $\dfrac{28}{5}$

4. The fraction $\dfrac{23}{4}$ is between the two positive integers (   ).

    A. 3 and 4   **B.** 4 and 5   **C.** 5 and 6   **D.** 6 and 7

5. Calculate.

    a. $2\dfrac{1}{3} + 3\dfrac{1}{4}$ **b.** $\dfrac{11}{3} - 1\dfrac{1}{2}$ **c.** $4\dfrac{2}{5} - 2\dfrac{1}{6}$

Example 7

I think of a number, subtract $\dfrac{2}{5}$ and then add $\dfrac{1}{4}$ and the result is $\dfrac{5}{8}$. What is my number?

Solution

Suppose my number is x, then write a number sentence.

$$x - \dfrac{2}{5} + \dfrac{1}{4} = \dfrac{5}{8}$$

$$x = \dfrac{5}{8} - \dfrac{1}{4} + \dfrac{2}{5}$$

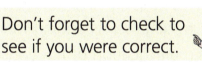

Don't forget to check to see if you were correct.

$$x = \dfrac{3}{8} + \dfrac{2}{5}$$

$$x = \dfrac{31}{40}$$

So my number is $\dfrac{31}{40}$.

Practice 2.4 (3)

1. Solve these equations.

    a. $x + \dfrac{2}{3} = \dfrac{1}{12} + \dfrac{3}{4}$ **b.** $x + \dfrac{3}{10} = \dfrac{4}{5} - \dfrac{1}{6}$

    c. $x - 1\dfrac{2}{7} = \dfrac{3}{14}$ **d.** $x - \dfrac{5}{3} = \dfrac{5}{6} + \dfrac{2}{9}$

2. Dylan spent $\dfrac{1}{3}$ hour doing his science homework, $\dfrac{1}{2}$ hour doing his Maths homework and $\dfrac{5}{12}$ hours doing his English homework. How many hours did he spend on his homework?

3. Year 6 pupils were invited to participate in science projects, but each pupil could take part in only one of them. $\frac{3}{100}$ of the whole year participated in the nature project, $\frac{3}{50}$ of the whole year participated in

the computing project and $\frac{7}{150}$ of the year participated in the maths project. What fraction of the whole year took part in the three projects altogether?

2.5 Multiplication of fractions

Think!

You know how to multiply positive integers, for example 4 × 2, which means adding four lots of 2. But what does multiplication of fractions mean? For example, how would you work out $\frac{4}{5} \times \frac{2}{3}$?

The diagram shows a square, with a side length of 1, divided vertically into 5 equal parts. Four of them are shaded pink. The pink region occupies $\frac{4}{5}$ of the original square. The square is then divided horizontally into 3 equal parts. What happens if the top two parts are shaded blue?

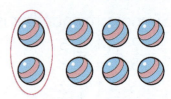

The top two parts of the pink region will turn purple. This purple region represents $\frac{4}{5} \times \frac{2}{3}$ of the original square.

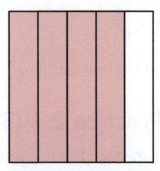

You can see that the purple region occupies $\frac{8}{15}$ of the square, which also means $\frac{4}{5} \times \frac{2}{3} = \frac{8}{15}$.

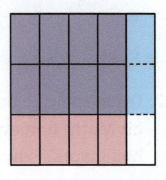

Generally, $\frac{p}{q}$ means dividing a whole into q equal parts and taking p of these parts. So the multiplication of two fractions $\left(\frac{p}{q} \times \frac{m}{n}\right)$ means taking $\frac{p}{q}$ as a whole, then dividing it into n parts and taking m parts of these. The result is $\frac{p \times m}{q \times n}$. It means that $\frac{p}{q} \times \frac{m}{n} = \frac{p \times m}{q \times n}$ ($q \neq 0$, $n \neq 0$).

To multiply two fractions, multiply the two numerators to get the new numerator, and multiply the two denominators to get the new denominator.

Example 1 Calculate.

a. $\frac{5}{6} \times \frac{1}{3}$ **b.** $\frac{3}{8} \times \frac{2}{5}$ **c.** $\frac{4}{9} \times 13\frac{1}{2}$

Solution

a. $\frac{5}{6} \times \frac{1}{3} = \frac{5 \times 1}{6 \times 3} = \frac{5}{18}$

b. $\frac{3}{8} \times \frac{2}{5} = \frac{3 \times 2}{8 \times 5} = \frac{6}{40} = \frac{3}{20}$

c. $\frac{4}{9} \times 13\frac{1}{2} = \frac{4}{9} \times \frac{27}{2} = \frac{108}{18} = 6$ ⟵ Turn mixed numbers into improper fractions first.

In parts **b.** and **c.**, the common factor can be cancelled before multiplication.

$$\frac{3}{\overset{}{\underset{4}{8}}} \times \frac{\overset{1}{2}}{5} = \frac{3 \times 1}{4 \times 5} = \frac{3}{20}$$

$$\frac{\overset{2}{4}}{\underset{1}{9}} \times \frac{\overset{3}{27}}{\underset{1}{2}} = 2 \times 3 = 6$$

I play the piano for $\frac{3}{4}$ hour every day. Do you know how many hours I play the piano in a week (7 days) altogether?

This means calculating seven times $\frac{3}{4}$ hour, but how can we calculate $\frac{3}{4} \times 7$?

When calculating $\frac{3}{4} \times 7$, write the integer 7 as the fraction $\frac{7}{1}$, so its denominator is 1, then $\frac{3}{4} \times 7 = \frac{3}{4} \times \frac{7}{1} = \frac{21}{4} = 5\frac{1}{4}$.

Similarly, $7 \times \frac{3}{4} = \frac{7}{1} \times \frac{3}{4} = \frac{21}{4} = 5\frac{1}{4}$.

When multiplying integers and fractions, the numerator of the product is obtained by multiplying the integer and the numerator of the fraction, and the denominator doesn't change.

Example 2 Calculate.

a. $\frac{5}{12} \times 6$ **b.** $12 \times \frac{3}{10}$

The common factor can be cancelled before multiplication.

Solution

a. $\frac{5}{12} \times 6 = \frac{5 \times 1}{2} = \frac{5}{2} = 2\frac{1}{2}$ **b.** $12 \times \frac{3}{10} = 6 \times \frac{3}{5} = \frac{18}{5} = 3\frac{3}{5}$

Example 3 Calculate.

a. $\frac{10}{3} \times 1\frac{1}{5}$ **b.** $3\frac{5}{12} \times 2\frac{3}{4}$

Solution

a. $\frac{10}{3} \times 1\frac{1}{5} = \frac{10}{3} \times \frac{6}{5} = 4$

b. $3\frac{5}{12} \times 2\frac{3}{4} = \frac{41}{12} \times \frac{11}{4} = \frac{451}{48} = 9\frac{19}{48}$

Example 4

A container holds 20 tonnes of goods. $\frac{5}{12}$ of the goods are clothes and children's clothing makes up $\frac{3}{8}$ of these. How many tonnes of children's clothing are there in this container?

Solution

$20 \times \frac{5}{12} = \frac{25}{3}$

> Work this out as 20 times $\frac{5}{12}$, the calculation is then $20 \times \frac{5}{12}$.

$\frac{25}{3} \times \frac{3}{8} = \frac{25}{8} = 3\frac{1}{8}$ (tonnes)

There are $3\frac{1}{8}$ tonnes of children's clothing in the container.

> Work this out as $\frac{25}{3}$ times $\frac{3}{8}$, the calculation is then $\frac{25}{3} \times \frac{3}{8}$.

A shorter way of showing the calculation is:

$20 \times \frac{5}{12} \times \frac{3}{8} = \frac{25}{8} = 3\frac{1}{8}$

Practice 2.5

1. Calculate these mentally.

  a. $\frac{1}{2} \times \frac{1}{3}$ 　　　 **b.** $\frac{2}{3} \times \frac{1}{5}$ 　　　 **c.** $\frac{3}{8} \times \frac{2}{3}$

  d. $\frac{5}{4} \times \frac{3}{4}$ 　　　 **e.** $4 \times \frac{5}{8}$ 　　　 **f.** $\frac{1}{3} \times 9$

2. Calculate.

  a. $\frac{12}{13} \times 2$ 　　　 **b.** $\frac{4}{7} \times 14$ 　　　 **c.** $8 \times \frac{5}{6}$

  d. $2\frac{3}{4} \times 3$ 　　　 **e.** $1\frac{2}{5} \times 2\frac{1}{3}$ 　　　 **f.** $\frac{3}{4} \times \frac{3}{4}$

3. Emma watches TV for $\frac{5}{6}$ hours every day. How many hours does she watch TV in 5 days?

4. The side length of a square is $\frac{5}{6}$ metres. How long is its perimeter?

5. a. How many kilograms is $\frac{1}{4}$ of $\frac{2}{3}$ kilograms?

  b. How many metres in is $\frac{2}{3}$ of $\frac{3}{8}$ metres?

    c. How many hours is $\dfrac{7}{24}$ of $\dfrac{12}{5}$ hours?

    d. How many metres is $\dfrac{3}{4}$ of $2\dfrac{2}{5}$ metres?

6. Write >, < or = in the brackets.

    a. $11 \times \dfrac{12}{13}$ ( ) $\dfrac{12}{13}$ **b.** $\dfrac{2}{3} \times \dfrac{4}{5}$ ( ) $\dfrac{2}{3}$

    c. $\dfrac{3}{5} \times 3$ ( ) $\dfrac{3}{5}$ **d.** $\dfrac{2}{11} \times \dfrac{12}{7}$ ( ) $\dfrac{2}{11}$

    Discuss how you can make the comparison above quickly.

7. Emma's family bought 25 kilograms of rice at the beginning of this month. They have $\dfrac{2}{5}$ of this left at the end of the month. How many kilograms of rice do they have at the end of the month?

2.6 Division of fractions

Think!

Mental calculation.

    a. $4 \times \dfrac{1}{4}$ **b.** $\dfrac{5}{12} \times \dfrac{12}{5}$

    c. $2\dfrac{2}{3} \times \dfrac{3}{8}$ **d.** $\dfrac{p}{q} \times \dfrac{q}{p}$ $(p \neq 0, q \neq 0)$

All the products of the multiplications of the two numbers are 1.

Based on your results, what conclusion can you make?

Just as for division of integers, division of fractions is the inverse operation of multiplication.

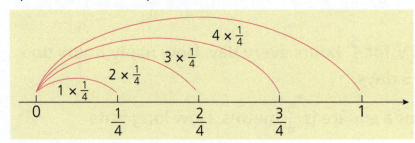

Because $4 \times \dfrac{1}{4} = 1$, so $1 \div \dfrac{1}{4} = 4$.

Because $\dfrac{p}{q} \times \dfrac{q}{p} = 1$, so $1 \div \dfrac{p}{q} = \dfrac{q}{p}$ $(p \neq 0, q \neq 0)$.

The quotient of a number (other than 0) is the result of dividing it into 1. This is called the **reciprocal** of that number.

The reciprocal of a is $\frac{1}{a}$ $(a \neq 0)$ and the reciprocal of $\frac{p}{q}$ is $\frac{q}{p}$ $(p \neq 0, q \neq 0)$.

The reciprocal of 4 is $\frac{1}{4}$, the reciprocal of $\frac{1}{4}$ is 4, 4 and $\frac{1}{4}$ are reciprocals of each other.

The reciprocal of $\frac{5}{12}$ is $\frac{12}{5}$, the reciprocal of $\frac{12}{5}$ is $\frac{5}{12}$, $\frac{5}{12}$ and $\frac{12}{5}$ are reciprocals of each other.

The product of two numbers that are reciprocals of each other is 1.

Does 0 have a reciprocal?
What is the reciprocal of 1?

? Problem

Find two numbers that are reciprocals of each other. Is it always true that one of them is larger than 1?

Practice 2.6 (1)

1. Write the reciprocal of each number.

$\frac{5}{6}$, $\frac{11}{4}$, 3, $2\frac{1}{2}$, b $(b \neq 0)$

2.

 All the numbers have reciprocals.

Surely two different numbers that are reciprocals of each other aren't equal.

Are these statements true or false?

Division is the inverse operation of multiplication.

$\longrightarrow$ By multiplication of fractions $\frac{2}{3} \times \frac{4}{5} = \frac{8}{15}$, the quotient of $\frac{8}{15}$ divided by $\frac{4}{5}$ is $\frac{2}{3}$. It is written as $\frac{8}{15} \div \frac{4}{5} = \frac{2}{3}$.

Think!

How can you calculate $\frac{2}{5} \div \frac{3}{4}$?

Suppose that $\frac{2}{5}$ divided by $\frac{3}{4}$ is x.

Then the equation will be $\frac{3}{4}x = \frac{2}{5}$.

> What is the equation? How can you solve the equation $\frac{3}{4}x = \frac{2}{5}$?

Multiplying both sides of the equation by $\frac{4}{3}$, which is the reciprocal of $\frac{3}{4}$:

$$\frac{4}{3} \times \frac{3}{4}x = \frac{2}{5} \times \frac{4}{3}$$

So $x = \frac{2}{5} \times \frac{4}{3}$, $x = \frac{8}{15}$.

Since $x = \frac{2}{5} \div \frac{3}{4}$, $\boxed{\frac{2}{5} \div \frac{3}{4} = \frac{2}{5} \times \frac{4}{3}}$

reciprocal

Based on the formula in the red box, what conclusion can you make?

Summary

> **The rule for division of fractions**
>
> A divided by B ($B \neq 0$) is equal to A multiplied by the reciprocal of B.
>
> In algebraic form: $\frac{m}{n} \div \frac{p}{q} = \frac{m}{n} \times \frac{q}{p}$ ($n \neq 0$, $p \neq 0$, $q \neq 0$).

Example 1 Poppy's home is 4 kilometres from the school. It takes $\frac{4}{11}$ hours to ride her bike to school.

What is Poppy's average speed on her bike, in kilometres per hour?

Solution $4 \div \frac{4}{11} = \overset{1}{4} \times \frac{11}{\underset{1}{4}} = 11$ (km/h)

Poppy's average speed riding her bike is 11 kilometres per hour.

Example 2 Calculate.

a. $\dfrac{15}{28} \div \dfrac{5}{7}$ 　　　　**b.** $\dfrac{4}{15} \div 8$ 　　　　**c.** $2\dfrac{1}{3} \div \dfrac{14}{15}$

Solution

a. $\dfrac{15}{28} \div \dfrac{5}{7} = \dfrac{\overset{3}{\cancel{15}}}{\underset{4}{\cancel{28}}} \times \dfrac{\overset{1}{\cancel{7}}}{\underset{1}{\cancel{5}}} = \dfrac{3}{4}$

How can we calculate this?

b. $\dfrac{4}{15} \div 8 = \dfrac{\overset{1}{\cancel{4}}}{15} \times \dfrac{1}{\underset{2}{\cancel{8}}} = \dfrac{1}{30}$

c. $2\dfrac{1}{3} \div \dfrac{14}{15} = \dfrac{7}{3} \div \dfrac{14}{15}$

$= \dfrac{\overset{1}{\cancel{7}}}{\underset{1}{\cancel{3}}} \times \dfrac{\overset{5}{\cancel{15}}}{\underset{2}{\cancel{14}}} = \dfrac{5}{2} = 2\dfrac{1}{2}$

Convert mixed numbers to improper fractions and then calculate.

Example 3 If $\dfrac{11}{12}$ times a number is $\dfrac{1}{3}$, what is the number?

Solution Let the number be x and write an equation based on the statement above: $\dfrac{11}{12} x = \dfrac{1}{3}$

$x = \dfrac{1}{3} \div \dfrac{11}{12},\quad x = \dfrac{1}{\underset{1}{\cancel{3}}} \times \dfrac{\overset{4}{\cancel{12}}}{11},\quad x = \dfrac{4}{11}$ 　So, this number is $\dfrac{4}{11}$.

Practice 2.6 (2)

1. Fill in the brackets.

a. $\dfrac{8}{9} \div \dfrac{2}{3} = \dfrac{8}{9} \times (\quad)$ 　　　　**b.** $\dfrac{11}{12} \div (\quad) = \dfrac{11}{12} \times \dfrac{3}{5}$

c. $\dfrac{2}{7} \div \dfrac{2}{5} = (\quad) \times \dfrac{5}{2}$ 　　　　**d.** $(\quad) \div \dfrac{13}{10} = \dfrac{3}{2} \times \dfrac{10}{13}$

2. Calculate.

a. $1 \div \dfrac{3}{8}$ 　　　**b.** $5 \div \dfrac{5}{6}$ 　　　**c.** $8 \div \dfrac{4}{5}$

d. $\dfrac{4}{5} \div 6$ 　　　**e.** $\dfrac{8}{9} \div \dfrac{1}{2}$ 　　　**f.** $\dfrac{2}{3} \div \dfrac{5}{2}$

3. Emma spent $\frac{8}{15}$ hours walking $\frac{8}{9}$ km. How many kilometres can she walk in an hour if she continues to walk at this speed?

4. Calculate.

   a. $\frac{4}{5} \div \frac{2}{3}$ b. $\frac{3}{11} \div \frac{2}{5}$ c. $\frac{5}{6} \div \frac{6}{5}$

   d. $\frac{2}{27} \div \frac{8}{9}$ e. $\frac{3}{10} \div \frac{6}{25}$ f. $\frac{5}{14} \div \frac{10}{7}$

5. Solve the equations.

   a. $\frac{6}{7}x = 3$ b. $\frac{5}{4}x = \frac{7}{8}$ c. $\frac{7}{24}x = \frac{2}{21}$

2.7 Converting between fractions and decimals

? The diameters of Mercury, Mars and the Moon are about $\frac{19}{50}$, $\frac{1}{2}$ and $\frac{869}{3189}$ of the diameter of Earth. Compare the diameters of these three celestial bodies.

You learned about fractions and decimals in earlier years and now you have learned the relationship between fractions and division. You can compare the three fractions above by reducing the fractions to a common denominator. You can also convert the fractions to decimals and then compare directly. For example, to compare $\frac{2}{5}$ with $\frac{3}{4}$, you can convert the fractions to decimals rather than reducing fractions to a common denominator.

$\frac{2}{5} = 2 \div 5 = 0.4$, $\frac{3}{4} = 3 \div 4 = 0.75$.

Since $0.4 < 0.75$, $\frac{2}{5} < \frac{3}{4}$.

Example 1

Convert these fractions to finite (terminating) decimals. If the fraction does not produce a finite decimal, round the result to the nearest thousandth.

$$\frac{3}{5}, \frac{4}{27}, \frac{16}{25}, \frac{31}{4}, \frac{9}{37}, \frac{17}{100}$$

$$\frac{4}{27} = 4 \div 27 = 0.148\,148\ldots$$

Solution

$$\frac{3}{5} = 3 \div 5 = 0.6, \quad \frac{4}{27} = 4 \div 27 \approx 0.148, \quad \frac{16}{25} = 16 \div 25 = 0.64$$

$$\frac{31}{4} = 31 \div 4 = 7.75, \quad \frac{9}{37} = 9 \div 37 \approx 0.243, \quad \frac{17}{100} = 17 \div 100 = 0.17$$

Work in groups. Use a calculator to convert some fractions to decimals. Can you find a rule for it?

> If the denominator of a fraction in its lowest terms only has prime factors 2 and 5, it can be converted directly to a terminating decimal. Otherwise, it can't be converted.

Can $\frac{5}{6}, \frac{3}{8}$ and $\frac{2}{15}$ be converted to terminating decimals?

Example 2

Convert 0.9, 0.25, 0.234 and 2.12 to fractions.

Solution

$$0.9 = \frac{9}{10}$$

0.9 has 1 decimal place. There are 9 tenths.

$$0.25 = \frac{25}{100} = \frac{1}{4}$$

0.25 has 2 decimal places. There are 25 hundredths.

$$0.234 = \frac{234}{1000} = \frac{117}{500}$$

0.234 has 3 decimal places. There are 234 thousandths.

2.12 has 2 decimal places. There are 212 hundredths.

$$2.12 = \frac{212}{100} = \frac{53}{25} = 2\frac{3}{25}$$

$$2.12 = 2 + \frac{1}{10} + \frac{2}{100} = \frac{212}{100} = \frac{53}{25}$$

Did you find an easier way to convert decimals to fractions, from the example above?

Generally, when you convert a decimal to a fraction, your final answer should be a fraction in its simplest form.

Example 3

Arrange $\frac{2}{5}$, $\frac{19}{40}$ and 0.45 in order from smallest to greatest.

Solution

$\frac{2}{5} = 0.4$, $\frac{19}{40} = 0.475$

Since $0.4 < 0.45 < 0.475$, the order should be $\frac{2}{5}$, 0.45, $\frac{19}{40}$.

Can you find another method to compare them?

Practice 2.7 (1)

1. **Convert these fractions to decimals. If the decimal does not terminate, round it to the nearest thousandth.**

   $\frac{7}{8}$, $\frac{4}{15}$, $\frac{12}{25}$, $\frac{5}{12}$, $\frac{17}{40}$, $\frac{32}{5}$, $\frac{45}{31}$

2. **Of these fractions, the one that is closest to 0.27 is (   ).**

   A. $\frac{1}{3}$ **B.** $\frac{4}{11}$ **C.** $\frac{7}{20}$ **D.** $\frac{11}{40}$

3. **Convert these decimals to fractions in their simplest form.**

   0.22, 0.15, 0.4, 0.32, 0.45, 0.65, 1.34, 2.56

4. **Arrange $\frac{4}{5}$, 0.75, $\frac{5}{8}$ and $\frac{15}{19}$ in order from greatest to smallest.**

5. **A nut on Dylan's bicycle has come loose and he wants to use a spanner to tighten it.**

   He has a set of spanners, with sizes $\frac{7}{64}$", $\frac{1}{8}$", $\frac{3}{32}$", $\frac{3}{16}$", $\frac{5}{32}$" and $\frac{1}{4}$".

   The $\frac{3}{32}$" spanner is too small and $\frac{3}{16}$" is too big. So Dylan has to choose a size between $\frac{3}{32}$" and $\frac{3}{16}$".

   Which sizes can he choose?*

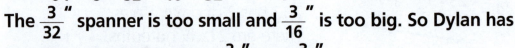

* $\frac{3}{32}$" means $\frac{3}{32}$ inch. An inch is a unit of length that was commonly used in the UK. It is part of the Imperial system of measures, which includes feet and miles. 1 inch is approximately 2.54 centimetres. Many lengths are now measured in the metric system, using kilometres, metres, centimetres and so on but road distances are still measured in miles.

Observation

Here's how to convert $\frac{1}{3}$ and $\frac{3}{22}$ to decimals.

```
      0.333...              0.13636...
   3)10               22)30
      9                   22
     ---                  ---
     10                    80
      9                    66
     ---                  ---
     10                   140
      9                   132
     ---                  ---
      1                    80
     ...                   66
                          ---
                          140
                          132
                          ---
                            8
                          ...
```

When will it end?

Can you find some rules?

In each fraction, when the numerator is divided by its denominator, it leaves a remainder. Some fractions give decimals that have a repeating set of digits after the decimal point in the quotient, for example:

The result of converting $\frac{1}{3}$ to a decimal is 0.3333... ←——— The repeating number is 3.

The result of converting $\frac{3}{22}$ to a decimal is 0.136 363 6... ←——— The repeating numbers are 36.

> The quotient is a repeating, or recurring, decimal. After a particular place after the decimal point, one number or a group of numbers repeats over and over again.
>
> The **repetend** of a recurring decimal is the set of digits (from first to last) that repeats for ever, after the decimal point.

To write recurring decimals more simply, you just write the first repetend, then write a dot above the first digit and the last one. For example:

The repetend of 0.3333... is 3.

You can write it as 0.3̇. So $\frac{1}{3}$ = 0.3̇.

The repetend of 0.136 363 6... is 36.

You can write it as 0.13̇6̇. So $\frac{3}{22}$ = 0.13̇6̇.

The repetend of 8.347 564 756… is 4756.
You can write it as 8.347̇ 56̇.

Example 4
Convert these fractions to recurring decimals.

a. $\frac{2}{9}$ b. $\frac{17}{22}$ c. $\frac{41}{27}$

Solution

a. $\frac{2}{9} = 0.\dot{2}$

> Why is the repetend not 772?

b. $\frac{17}{22} = 0.7\dot{7}\dot{2}$

c. $\frac{41}{27} = 1.\dot{5}1\dot{8}$

A fraction can always be converted to a finite decimal or a recurring decimal. Finite decimals or recurring decimals can be converted to fractions. (Converting recurring decimals to fractions is explained in the extension activity on the next page.)

Practice 2.7 (2)

1. **Which of these are recurring decimals? Which are not?**
   0.555, 0.123 123…, 1.234 5345…
   2.235 464 309…, 0.210 210…, 12.121 212…

2. **The repetend of the recurring decimal 2.357 57… is _____. It can be written in a simple form as _____. It can be written rounded to the nearest thousandth as _____.**

3. **Convert these fractions to decimals.**
   a. $\frac{5}{9}$ b. $\frac{9}{5}$ c. $\frac{11}{12}$ d. $\frac{43}{11}$

4. **Arrange $\frac{2}{3}$, 0.666, 0.665̇7̇ in order from smallest to greatest.**

5. **Now can you compare the diameters of Mercury, Mars and the Moon (see page 58)?**

Extension activity: Converting between recurring decimals and fractions

All fractions can be converted to decimals by dividing the numerator by the denominator. When it is an exact division, the decimal is a **finite decimal**. When the quotient has a remainder, the decimal is an **infinite recurring decimal**. Finite decimals and infinite recurring decimals can be converted to fractions. You have learned how to convert finite decimals to fractions, but how can you convert infinite recurring decimals to fractions?

You will learn more about it in your later mathematical studies. Here, you will just learn one solution.

Example 1 Convert $0.\dot{5}$ to a fraction.

Solution Let $x = 0.\dot{5}$, then $10x = 5.\dot{5}$.

$5.\dot{5} = 5 + 0.\dot{5}$, so $10x = 5 + x$.

The equation can be simplified to $9x = 5$, $x = \dfrac{5}{9}$.

So, $0.\dot{5} = \dfrac{5}{9}$.

Example 2 Convert $0.\dot{5}\dot{3}$ to a fraction.

Solution Let $x = 0.\dot{5}\dot{3}$, then $100x = 53.\dot{5}\dot{3}$.

$53.\dot{5}\dot{3} = 53 + 0.\dot{5}\dot{3}$, so $100x = 53 + x$.

$$53 + 0.\dot{5}\dot{3} = 53 + x$$

The equation can be simplified to $99x = 53$, $x = \dfrac{53}{99}$.

So, $0.\dot{5}\dot{3} = \dfrac{53}{99}$.

Example 3 Convert $0.1\dot{5}0\dot{3}$ to a fraction.

Solution Let $x = 0.\dot{5}0\dot{3}$, then $1000x = 503.\dot{5}0\dot{3}$.

$503.\dot{5}0\dot{3} = 503 + 0.\dot{5}0\dot{3}$, so $1000x = 503 + x$.

The equation can be simplified to $999x = 503$, $x = \dfrac{503}{999}$.

Now $0.1\dot{5}0\dot{3} = 0.1 + 0.0\dot{5}0\dot{3}$

and $0.1 + 0.0\dot{5}0\dot{3} = \dfrac{1+x}{10}$

So, $0.1\dot{5}0\dot{3} = \dfrac{1\,502}{9990} = \dfrac{751}{4995}$.

How do we get the equation

$0.1 + 0.0\dot{5}0\dot{3} = \dfrac{1+x}{10}$?

Think!

Using the method above, convert the infinite recurring decimal $0.\dot{9}$ to a fraction.

What do you find? Are you surprised at the result?

$0.\dot{9} = 1$

2.8 Mixed operations with fractions and decimals

The order in which you carry out mixed operations with fractions and decimals is the same as for integers.

Example 1 Calculate.

    a. $\dfrac{3}{4} - 0.25$

    b. $\dfrac{2}{3} + 0.55$

Analysis These are operations of addition and subtraction on fractions and decimals. You just need to make sure that both numbers in the question are either fractions or decimals, then calculate the answer. When a fraction cannot be converted into a finite decimal, convert the decimal to a fraction instead.

Solution **a.** $\dfrac{3}{4} - 0.25 = 0.75 - 0.25 = 0.5$

        or $\dfrac{3}{4} - 0.25 = \dfrac{3}{4} - \dfrac{1}{4} = \dfrac{1}{2}$

    b. $\dfrac{2}{3} + 0.55 = \dfrac{2}{3} + \dfrac{55}{100} = \dfrac{2}{3} + \dfrac{11}{20}$

        $= \dfrac{40 + 33}{60} = \dfrac{73}{60} = 1\dfrac{13}{60}$

Example 2 A group of young people go on an outing to a forest trail.

The whole trip takes $5\frac{3}{4}$ hours. The bus journey takes them 2 hours and 10 minutes and they spend 0.5 hours having lunch.

How many hours do they actually spend at the forest trail?

Analysis 2 hours and 10 minutes can be converted into $2\frac{1}{6}$ hours.

Solution
$$5\frac{3}{4} - 2\frac{1}{6} - 0.5$$
$$= 5 + \frac{3}{4} - 2 - \frac{1}{6} - \frac{1}{2}$$
$$= 3 + \frac{9}{12} - \frac{2}{12} - \frac{6}{12}$$
$$= 3 + \frac{1}{12}$$
$$= 3\frac{1}{12} \text{ (hours)}$$

The actual time that they spend at the forest trail is $3\frac{1}{12}$ hours.

It can also be calculated this way:
$$5\frac{3}{4} - 2\frac{1}{6} - 0.5$$
$$= 3 + \frac{3}{4} - \frac{1}{6} - \frac{1}{2}$$
$$= 3 + \frac{3}{4} - \left(\frac{1}{6} + \frac{1}{2}\right)$$
$$= 3 + \frac{3}{4} - \frac{2}{3}$$
$$= 3 + \frac{9-8}{12}$$
$$= 3\frac{1}{12}$$

 # Think!

Calculate: $\frac{3}{8} \div 3 \times \frac{3}{4}$

$$\frac{3}{8} \div 3 \times \frac{3}{4} = \frac{9}{8} \times \frac{3}{4} = \frac{27}{32}$$

$$\frac{3}{8} \div 3 \times \frac{3}{4} = \frac{3}{8} \div \left(3 \times \frac{3}{4}\right)$$
$$= \frac{3}{8} \div \frac{9}{4} = \frac{3}{8} \times \frac{4}{9} = \frac{1}{6}$$

Are their solutions right or not? If either is wrong, say why and correct it.

Example 3 Calculate.

    a. $\frac{12}{25} \div \frac{2}{3} \div \frac{6}{5}$ **b.** $\frac{3}{7} \times \frac{5}{6} + \frac{5}{14} \div \frac{2}{3}$

Solution   **a.** $\frac{12}{25} \div \frac{2}{3} \div \frac{6}{5}$

$$= \frac{\overset{6}{\cancel{12}}}{25} \times \frac{3}{\underset{1}{\cancel{2}}} \div \frac{6}{5}$$

$$= \frac{\overset{1}{\cancel{6}}}{\underset{5}{\cancel{25}}} \times 3 \times \frac{\overset{1}{\cancel{5}}}{\underset{1}{\cancel{6}}}$$

$$= \frac{3}{5}$$

> You must convert division into multiplication first, then cancel.
>
> $$\frac{12}{25} \div \frac{2}{3} \div \frac{6}{5}$$
>
> $$= \frac{12}{25} \times \frac{3}{2} \times \frac{5}{6}$$

b. $\frac{3}{7} \times \frac{5}{6} + \frac{5}{14} \div \frac{2}{3}$

$$= \frac{\overset{1}{\cancel{3}}}{7} \times \frac{5}{\underset{2}{\cancel{6}}} + \frac{5}{14} \times \frac{3}{2}$$

$$= \frac{5}{14} + \frac{15}{28} = \frac{25}{28}$$

> First do multiplication and division, and then do addition and subtraction.

Example 4 Calculate: $\frac{3}{4} \times \left(2.5 - \frac{1}{4}\right) + \frac{5}{12} \div 0.25$

> Convert decimals into fractions first, and then calculate.

Solution $\frac{3}{4} \times \left(2.5 - \frac{1}{4}\right) + \frac{5}{12} \div 0.25$

$$= \frac{3}{4} \times \frac{10 - 1}{4} + \frac{5}{12} \div \frac{1}{4}$$

$$= \frac{27}{16} + \frac{5}{12} \times 4 = \frac{81 + 80}{48} = \frac{161}{48} = 3\frac{17}{48}$$

Example 5 In a supermarket, the cost of oranges is £1.80 per kilogram. Poppy bought 5 kilograms, and Emma bought $\frac{3}{4}$ as many as Poppy. Emma gives the shop assistant £50. How much change does the shop assistant give Emma?

Solution Emma buys: $5 \times \frac{3}{4} = \frac{15}{4}$ kg of oranges.

Emma should pay:

$$\frac{15}{4} \times 1.8 = \frac{15}{4} \times \frac{9}{5} = \frac{135}{20}$$

$$= 6.75$$

$$10 - 6.75 = 3.25$$

The shop assistant should give Emma £3.25 change.

> You can also calculate directly:
>
> $$10 - 5 \times \frac{3}{4} \times 1.8$$
>
> $$= 10 - 5 \times \frac{3}{4} \times \frac{9}{5}$$
>
> $$= 3.25$$

Think!

Look at these operations.

$$\frac{2}{3} \times \left(\frac{5}{6} + \frac{3}{7}\right) = \frac{2}{3} \times \frac{35 + 18}{42} = \frac{53}{63}$$

$$\frac{2}{3} \times \frac{5}{6} + \frac{2}{3} \times \frac{3}{7} = \frac{5}{9} + \frac{2}{7} = \frac{35 + 18}{63} = \frac{53}{63}$$

Can you see a rule?

The distributive law of multiplication applies to fraction calculations.

Example 6 Calculate.

    a. $\frac{2}{3} \times \left(\frac{3}{8} + \frac{5}{6}\right)$ **b.** $\left(\frac{14}{15} - \frac{7}{24}\right) \times \frac{3}{2}$

Solution   **a.** $\frac{2}{3} \times \left(\frac{3}{8} + \frac{5}{6}\right)$

$$= \frac{2}{3} \times \frac{3}{8} + \frac{2}{3} \times \frac{5}{6} = \frac{1}{4} + \frac{5}{9} = \frac{29}{36}$$

    b. Method 1:

$$\left(\frac{14}{15} - \frac{7}{24}\right) \times \frac{3}{2}$$

$$= \frac{14}{15} \times \frac{3}{2} - \frac{7}{24} \times \frac{3}{2} = \frac{7}{5} - \frac{7}{16} = \frac{77}{80}$$

Method 2:

$$\left(\frac{14}{15} - \frac{7}{24}\right) \times \frac{3}{2}$$

$$= \left(\frac{2 \times 7}{5 \times 3} - \frac{1 \times 7}{8 \times 3}\right) \times \frac{3}{2}$$

$$= \left(\frac{2}{5} - \frac{1}{8}\right) \times \frac{7}{3} \times \frac{3}{2}$$

$$= \frac{11}{40} \times \frac{7}{2} = \frac{77}{80}$$

Why can $\frac{7}{3}$ be moved out of the brackets?

Practice 2.8

1. Calculate.

    a. $4 \times \frac{3}{11} \div \frac{3}{5}$ **b.** $\frac{3}{4} \times \frac{5}{12} \div \frac{2}{5}$

    c. $\frac{5}{12} \div \frac{3}{4} \div \frac{1}{3}$ **d.** $\frac{9}{10} \div \frac{2}{5} \times \frac{3}{8}$

2. Calculate.

a. $\dfrac{3}{5} \times \dfrac{2}{3} + \dfrac{6}{7} \div \dfrac{3}{14}$ b. $2 \div \dfrac{3}{4} - \dfrac{3}{5} \times \dfrac{5}{9}$ c. $\dfrac{3}{4} \times \left(\dfrac{2}{5} - \dfrac{1}{3}\right) + \dfrac{7}{8} \div \dfrac{1}{2}$

3. Calculate.

a. $3.5 - \dfrac{2}{3} + \dfrac{3}{5}$ b. $1.25 \times \left(2\dfrac{2}{5} - \dfrac{1}{2}\right) + \dfrac{11}{10} \div 2$

c. $3.2 \times \dfrac{4}{5} \times \dfrac{7}{8}$ d. $2\dfrac{3}{5} \div \left(2.2 + \dfrac{1}{10}\right) + \dfrac{2}{3} \times 6.9$

4. The length of a picture is 9 cm and its width is 5.4 cm.
It is $\dfrac{1}{25}$ cm thick.

a. What is the area of the picture?

b. A stack of these pictures is 4.4 cm high. How many pictures are there in this stack?

5. Calculate.

a. $12 \times \left(\dfrac{5}{6} + \dfrac{11}{24}\right)$ b. $\dfrac{3}{4} \times \left(\dfrac{7}{12} - \dfrac{2}{9}\right)$

2.9 Applications of fraction operations

Example 1   Poppy plans to spend three days reading a book. She reads $\dfrac{2}{7}$ of it the first day and $\dfrac{3}{5}$ of it the second day.
What fraction of the book does Poppy read on the third day, to finish it?

Analysis   Treat the book as a whole, and use 1 to represent it.
She reads $\dfrac{2}{7} + \dfrac{3}{5}$ of it in two days. Subtract the total (the amount read in the previous two days) from 1 to find the required answer.

Solution $1 - 1 \times \left(\dfrac{2}{7} - \dfrac{3}{5}\right)$

It also can be
$1 - \dfrac{2}{7} - \dfrac{3}{5} = \dfrac{4}{35}$

$= 1 - \dfrac{31}{35} = \dfrac{35 - 31}{35} = \dfrac{4}{35}$

Poppy reads $\dfrac{4}{35}$ of the book on the third day.

Example 2 The surface of a football is made of black and white pieces of leather stitched together. You know that the number of black pieces is $\frac{3}{5}$ of the number of white pieces. If there are 12 pieces of black leather, what is the total number of black and white pieces of leather in the football?

Analysis First, find the number of white pieces of leather. From the fact that $\frac{3}{5}$ of the number of white pieces is equal to the number of black pieces, you can make the equation.

Solution Let x be the number of pieces of white leather. $\frac{3}{5}x = 12$

$x = 12 \div \frac{3}{5} = 12 \times \frac{5}{3} = 20$

$20 + 12 = 32$

There are 32 black and white pieces of leather stitched into the football.

Example 3 The price of housing plots in a community was originally £4200 per square metre. Now it has increased by $\frac{1}{100}$ of the original price.

a. What is the price per square metre now?

b. When anyone buys a house they need to pay $\frac{3}{200}$ of the total price as an extra tax. Based on the new rate, how much should Dylan's dad pay for a house with an area of 120 square metres?

Solution **a.** $4200 \times \frac{1}{100} = 42$, $4200 + 42 = 4242$
The current price per square metre is £4242.

b. $120 \times 4242 + 120 \times 4242 \times \frac{3}{200}$

$= 509\,040 + 509\,040 \times \frac{3}{200}$

$= 509\,040 + 2545.2 \times 3$

$= 516\,675.6$

The current price of a house with an area of 120 square metres is £516\,675.60.

Now return to the question at the beginning of this unit.

Yao Ming's height is 226 cm and his mass is 134 kg; Bateer's height is 210 cm and his mass is 130 kg. Dylan's height is $\frac{3}{5}$ of Yao Ming's height and his mass is $\frac{7}{20}$ of Yao Ming's mass. Emma's height is $\frac{5}{7}$ of Bateer's height and her mass is $\frac{9}{26}$ of Bateer's mass.

Who is taller, Dylan or Emma? Who is heavier?

Dylan's height: $226 \times \frac{3}{5} = 135.6$ (cm)

mass: $134 \times \frac{7}{20} = 46.9$ (kg)

Emma's height: $210 \times \frac{5}{7} = 150$ (cm)

mass: $130 \times \frac{9}{26} = 45$ (kg)

> Is there another way to compare Dylan's and Emma's heights and masses?

Therefore, Emma is taller than Dylan and Dylan is heavier than Emma.

Practice 2.9

1. $\frac{3}{7}$ of a number is equal to $\frac{2}{5}$ of 6. What is this number?

2. Solve the equations.

    a. $2x + \frac{1}{3} = 1$ **b.** $x + \frac{5}{7} = 2\frac{1}{2} \times \frac{1}{3}$

3. The volume of a cuboid is $\frac{16}{5}$ cubic metres. Its length is $\frac{4}{3}$ metres and its width is $\frac{1}{5}$ metre. What is the height of the cuboid?

4. Poppy's time for the 100 metres race is 14 seconds. Emma's time for the 100 metres race is $\frac{27}{28}$ of Poppy's time. Who runs faster? By how many seconds does she lead? If your time for the 100 metres race is 1.4 seconds faster than Poppy's, can you break the Year record for the 100 metres race of 12.7 seconds?

Unit summary

In this unit you have examined the concepts of fractions, addition, subtraction, multiplication and division of fractions, and the interaction and operations of fractions and decimals. Through the study of fractions, your ability to carry out operations and solve practical problems has improved. You have also learned about the mathematical way of thinking, in studying and solving fraction problems by converting the different denominators into common denominators.

The framework of this unit is shown below.

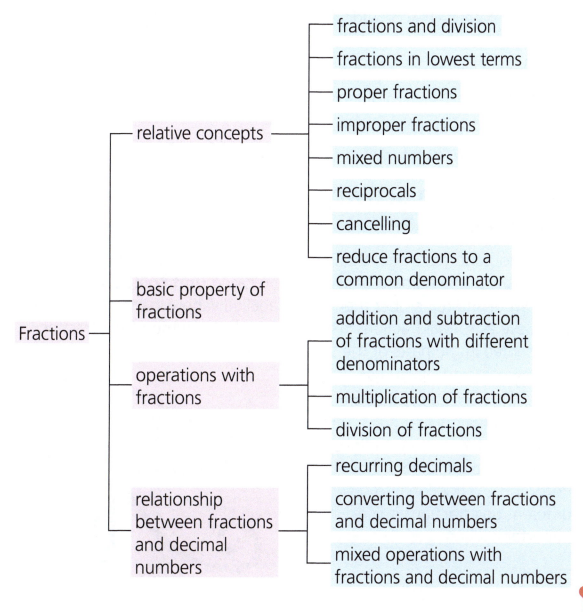

Investigation activity 1: Using a calculator to check operation laws

The operations of addition and multiplication of positive integers are the commutative law of addition, the associative law of addition, the commutative law of multiplication, the associative law of multiplication and the distributive law of multiplication.

The addition and multiplication of fractions and decimals obey these operation laws as well. Use a calculator to check this.

Operation law	Example	Check with a calculator
The commutative law of addition	$\frac{2}{3} + \frac{3}{4} = \frac{3}{4} + \frac{2}{3}$	
The associative law of addition		
The commutative law of multiplication		
The associative law of multiplication		
The distributive law of multiplication		

Investigation activity 2: Decomposition of fractions

Three thousand years ago, the Egyptians invented a method of writing fractions with the numerator 1. These are called **unit fractions**. To help them write and remember them, they labelled various parts of the sun-god's eye as special fractions. The diagram shows some of the fractions represented in the parts of the sun-god's eye.

The Egyptians calculated by converting numerators that are not 1 into numerators that are 1, which makes calculations very complicated. However, the question of how to decompose a fraction into several different unit fractions is very important.

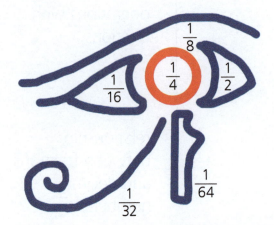

For example: $\dfrac{1}{2} = \dfrac{3}{6} = \dfrac{1+2}{6} = \dfrac{1}{6} + \dfrac{2}{6} = \dfrac{1}{6} + \dfrac{1}{3}$

$\dfrac{1}{3} = \dfrac{4}{12} = \dfrac{1+3}{12} = \dfrac{1}{12} + \dfrac{3}{12} = \dfrac{1}{12} + \dfrac{1}{4}$

$\dfrac{2}{3} = \dfrac{4}{6} = \dfrac{1+3}{6} = \dfrac{1}{6} + \dfrac{3}{6} = \dfrac{1}{6} + \dfrac{1}{2}$

$\dfrac{3}{5} = \dfrac{24}{40} = \dfrac{4+20}{40} = \dfrac{4}{40} + \dfrac{20}{40} = \dfrac{1}{10} + \dfrac{1}{2}$

or $\dfrac{3}{5} = \dfrac{9}{15} = \dfrac{1+3+5}{15} = \dfrac{1}{15} + \dfrac{3}{15} + \dfrac{5}{15} = \dfrac{1}{15} + \dfrac{1}{5} + \dfrac{1}{3}$

Similarly, 1 can also be decomposed into the sum of several different unit fractions, such as:

$$1 = \dfrac{3}{3} = \dfrac{1+2}{3} = \dfrac{1}{3} + \dfrac{2}{3} = \dfrac{1}{3} + \dfrac{4}{6} = \dfrac{1}{3} + \dfrac{1}{6} + \dfrac{1}{2}$$

Can you decompose 1 into the sum of several fractions with different denominators that are odd numbers? It is possible:

$$1 = \dfrac{1}{3} + \dfrac{1}{5} + \dfrac{1}{7} + \dfrac{1}{9} + \dfrac{1}{11} + \dfrac{1}{15} + \dfrac{1}{35} + \dfrac{1}{45} + \dfrac{1}{231}$$

However, this method is not unique. 1 also can be decomposed into:

$$1 = \dfrac{1}{3} + \dfrac{1}{5} + \dfrac{1}{7} + \dfrac{1}{9} + \dfrac{1}{11} + \dfrac{1}{15} + \dfrac{1}{21} + \dfrac{1}{165} + \dfrac{1}{693}$$

Try it out! Can you decompose 1 into the sum of several different unit fractions?

The above examples illustrate that a fraction can be decomposed into the sum of several different unit fractions. What's more, the method of decomposition is not unique. Now you have a try!

Decompose $\dfrac{3}{4}$, $\dfrac{2}{7}$, $\dfrac{7}{16}$ and $\dfrac{5}{27}$ into the sum of several different unit fractions.

Extra reading material: Fraction operations in ancient China

The ancient Chinese mathematical classic, *The Nine Chapters on the Mathematical Art*, describes in detail rules about fractions and methods of working with them. The fraction operations it covers are: cancelling, addition, subtraction, multiplication, division, comparing and averages.

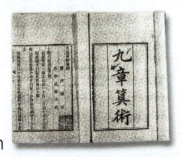

The method for cancelling fractions as explained in the ancient book is:

Halve any integer that can be exactly halved. If it cannot be halved exactly, compare the numerical sizes of the numerator and denominator. Then subtract the smaller one from the greater one again and again until they are equal. For the final step, the numerator and denominator are divided by an equal number.

If we translate this into modern English, we get:

If the numerator and denominator are both even numbers, they can both be halved, so divide both the numerator and denominator by 2 (cancel by 2).

If the numerator and/or the denominator is odd, so cannot be halved, compare the numerator and denominator. Subtract the smaller number from the greater number, and repeat until the two numbers are equal.

Finally, divide the original numerator and denominator by this number.

So, we can see that the Ancient Chinese method of cancelling fractions has three steps.

Let's try cancelling $\frac{15}{20}$: Because 15 is an odd number (which cannot be exactly halved), we subtract the smaller one from the greater one again and again until we get two numbers that are equal, so $(15, 20) \rightarrow (15, 5) \rightarrow (10, 5) \rightarrow (5, 5)$. This gives us the equal number 5. Then, to cancel, the numerator and denominator are divided by 5. This gives $\frac{15 \div 5}{20 \div 5} = \frac{3}{4}$.

Ha Fen means 'adding fractions'. We find the denominator by multiplying the denominators of the two starting fractions. We find the numerator by adding the product of each numerator multiplied by the denominator of the other fraction. Using letters to represent the numbers, we can write this as:

$$\frac{a}{b} + \frac{c}{d} = \frac{ad + bc}{bd}.$$

Chen Fen means 'multiplying fractions'. We find the denominator by multiplying the denominators of the two starting fractions. We find the numerator by multiplying the two numerators. Using letters to represent the numbers, we can write this as:

$$\frac{a}{b} \times \frac{c}{d} = \frac{ac}{bd}.$$

These ancient methods are the same as those you have learned.

Unit Three
Ratio and proportion

Section One: Ratio and proportion
3.1 The meaning of ratios

Think!

Dylan and Emma are having a basketball shoot-off in the basketball court. Dylan shoots 15 times and scores 6 baskets and Emma shoots 10 times and scores 5 baskets. Who has the better shooting skills?

Since 6 > 5, Dylan has better shooting skills than Emma.

Do you agree with Poppy?

The level of shooting skills is not only linked to goals but also to the number of shots.

$$\frac{\text{Dylan's number of goals}}{\text{Dylan's number of shots}} = \frac{6}{15} = \frac{2}{5}$$

$$\frac{\text{Emma's number of goals}}{\text{Emma's number of shots}} = \frac{5}{10} = \frac{1}{2}$$

We can use division to compare the relationship between two similar scales or two numbers.

Because $\frac{1}{2} > \frac{2}{5}$, Emma's shooting skills are better than Dylan's shooting skills.

Suppose *a* and *b* are two numbers. To compare *b* with *a*, you need to divide *a* by *b*. This is called the **ratio** of *a* and *b*, written as *a* : *b* or as $\frac{a}{b}$. Note: *b* must not be zero ($b \neq 0$).

You read it as '*a* compared to *b*' or 'the ratio of *a* to *b*'.

a is called the **first term** of the ratio and *b* is called the **second term** of the ratio. The **quotient** of the preceding item *a* divided by the latter item *b* is called the **value of the ratio**.

We can use ratios to compare two numbers, *a* and *b*. We can also write ratios as fractions.

Here are some examples of ratios.

The ratio of apples to oranges is 3 : 5. This can also be written as $\frac{3}{5}$.

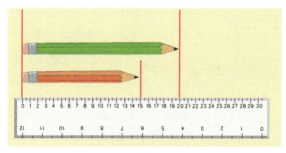

The ratio of the lengths of these two pencils is 20 : 15.

Can you think of any other examples of ratios?

Think!

In Unit Two, you learned about the relationship between fractions and division. Do you know the relationships between ratios, fractions and division?

> **The relationships between ratios, fractions and division**
> - The first term of the ratio corresponds to the numerator of the fraction and the dividend in division.
> - The second term of the ratio corresponds to the denominator of the fraction and the divisor in division.
> - The value of the ratio corresponds to the value of the fraction, and the quotient in division.

> Ratio: first term : second term = value of the ratio
> Fraction: numerator ÷ denominator = value of the fraction
> Division: dividend ÷ divisor = quotient

Example 1 What is the value of each ratio?

a. $36:6$ **b.** $1\frac{4}{5}:\frac{2}{7}$ **c.** $7.5\,\text{cm}:40\,\text{mm}$ **d.** 18 seconds : 1.5 minutes

Solution

a. $36:6 = 36 \div 6 = 6$

b. $1\frac{4}{5}:\frac{2}{7} = 1\frac{4}{5} \div \frac{2}{7} = \frac{9}{5} \times \frac{7}{2} = 6\frac{3}{10}$

c. $7.5\,\text{cm}:40\,\text{mm} = 75\,\text{mm} \div 40\,\text{mm} = 75 \div 40 = 1.875$

d. 18 seconds : 1.5 minutes
   = 18 seconds : 90 seconds
   = $18 \div 90 = 0.2$

> 1 minute = 60 seconds
> 1.5 minutes = 90 seconds

> If the units of the terms are different, you will need to convert both terms to the same units to find the ratio.

Practice 3.1

1. **There are 15 boys and 25 girls in Year 6 Class 5. Write the value of each ratio.**
   a. number of boys : number of girls
   b. number of boys : number of pupils in the whole class
   c. number of girls : number of pupils in the whole class

2. **Find the value of each of these ratios.**

   a. $9 : 15$
   b. $1.5 : 0.5$
   c. $2\frac{1}{2} : \frac{4}{5}$
   d. $75\,\text{g} : 0.5\,\text{kg}$

   e. $1.5\,\text{m} : 400\,\text{cm}$
   f. 5 hours : 160 minutes
   g. 16 hours : 5 days

3.2 Basic properties of ratios

 Think!

Poppy mixed 10 grams of concentrated fruit juice powder with 100 grams of water. Amelia dissolved 20 grams of the same concentrated fruit juice powder in 200 grams of water. Do the two fruit drinks taste the same?

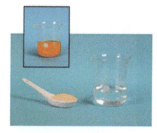

Mrs Richards dissolved 40 grams of the concentrated fruit juice powder in 400 grams of water. What does her fruit drink taste like, compared to the previous two?

Since $10 : 100 = 0.1$, $20 : 200 = 0.1$, $40 : 400 = 0.1$
then $10 : 100 = 20 : 200 = 40 : 400$

Therefore, the three fruit drinks all taste the same.

From the basic property of fractions, $\dfrac{a}{b} = \dfrac{ka}{kb} = \dfrac{a \div k}{b \div k}$ $(k \neq 0)$, you can conclude that

$$a : b = ka : kb = \frac{a}{k} : \frac{b}{k} \ (k \neq 0)$$

Summary

The basic property of ratios

If you multiply or divide both the first term and the second term of a ratio by the same number (apart from 0), the value of the ratio remains the same.

The simplest integer ratio means that both the first term and the second term of the ratio are integers and co-prime.

We can simplify ratios into integer values in their simplest form.

Example 1 Simplify these ratios.

a. $\dfrac{88}{132}$ **b.** $0.65 : 1.3$ **c.** $1\dfrac{1}{5} : \dfrac{3}{5}$ **d.** 1.25 litres : 375 millilitres

Solution

a. $\dfrac{88}{132} = \dfrac{88 \div 44}{132 \div 44} = \dfrac{2}{3}$

b. $0.65 : 1.3$
$= (0.65 \times 100) : (1.3 \times 100)$
$= 65 : 130$
$= 1 : 2$

c. $1\dfrac{1}{5} : \dfrac{3}{5}$

$= \dfrac{6}{5} : \dfrac{3}{5}$

$= \left(\dfrac{6}{5} \times 5\right) : \left(\dfrac{3}{5} \times 5\right)$

$= 6 : 3$

$= 2 : 1$

Or: $1\dfrac{1}{5} : \dfrac{3}{5} = \left(\dfrac{6}{5} \div \dfrac{3}{5}\right) : 1$

$= \left(\dfrac{6}{5} \times \dfrac{5}{3}\right) : 1 = 2 : 1$

d. 1.25 litres : 375 millilitres
$= 1250$ millilitres : 375 millilitres
$= (1250 \div 125) : (375 \div 125)$
$= 10 : 3$

1 litre = 1000 millilitres
1.25 litres = 1250 millilitres

Some of the ingredients for a cake recipe are 300 grams of cocoa powder, 100 grams of granulated sugar, 200 grams of milk powder. The ratio of cocoa powder to sugar is 300 : 100 or 3 : 1 and the ratio of sugar to milk powder is 100 : 200 or 1 : 2.

We can also say the ratio of cocoa to sugar to milk powder is 300 : 100 : 200. A ratio like this is called a **continued ratio of three terms** and 300, 100 and 200 are the terms of the continued ratio. When comparing two or more quantities, we will often use continued ratios.

The ratio of the heights of Dylan, Poppy and Emma is a continued ratio of the heights of three people.

We can work it out like this.

1.36 m : 1.45 m : 1.50 m
= 136 cm : 145 cm : 150 cm
= 136 : 145 : 150

Summary

The property of three consecutive ratios is:

If $a : b = m : n$ and $b : c = n : k$, $a : b : c = m : n : k$

If $k \neq 0$, $a : b : c = ak : bk : kc = \dfrac{a}{k} : \dfrac{b}{k} : \dfrac{c}{k}$

Example 2 **a.** Given $a : b = 2 : 3$ and $b : c = 3 : 5$, calculate $a : b : c$.

b. Given $a : b = 2 : 3$ and $b : c = 4 : 5$, calculate $a : b : c$.

Solution **a.** Since $a : b = 2 : 3$ and $b : c = 3 : 5$
then $a : b : c = 2 : 3 : 5$

Why do we need to convert 2 : 3 to 8 : 12?

b. $a : b = 2 : 3 = (2 \times 4) : (3 \times 4) \qquad = \qquad 8 : 12$

$b : c = 4 : 5 = \qquad (4 \times 3) : (5 \times 3) = 12 : 15$

So $a : b : c = 8 : 12 : 15$

81

✎ Practice 3.2

1. Simplify these ratios.

    a. $48:64$ **b.** $4.6:6.9$

    c. $220\,cm:1.1\,m$ **d.** $1.5\,l:750\,ml$

2. Work out the ratio of the mass of the white rabbit to the mass of the black rabbit.

3. Convert these continued ratios into simple integral ratios.

    a. $15:30:40$ **b.** $\dfrac{1}{2}:\dfrac{1}{4}:\dfrac{1}{6}$

4. Use the given conditions to work out $a:b:c$.

    a. $a:b = 5:3,\ b:c = 2:3$ **b.** $a:b = 4:5,\ b:c = 7:9$

3.3 Proportion

 Think!

Can you make a scale drawing of the top of your desk in your exercise book?

Suppose, after measuring carefully, you know that your desk is 1.2 metres long and 0.5 metres wide. You want to make a scale drawing of the top of your desk in your exercise book. It is not possible to draw it correctly at its actual size.

Using the basic property of ratio, you can use a scale of $1.2\,m:0.5\,m$ = $12\,cm:5\,cm$. Therefore, you can draw the top of your desk in your exercise book, representing its size of 1.2 metres long and 0.5 metres wide.

Are there any other ways of drawing it, apart from this scale?

Considering a, b, c and d, if $a:b = c:d$, then a, b, c and d are in **proportion**. The formula showing that the two ratios are equal is a statement of proportion. Also, a, b, c and d are the first proportion term, the second proportion term, the third proportion term and the fourth proportion term, respectively. As a is the first proportion term and d is the fourth proportion term, these outer terms a and d are called the **extremes** of the proportion. Then the inner terms b and c, as the second proportion term and the third proportion term, are called the **means** of the proportion.

If two means of a proportion are the same, b is called the **geometric mean** of a and c.

first proportion term
second proportion term
third proportion term
fourth proportion term

$1.2:0.5 = 12:5$

Also, 1.2 and 5 are the extremes of the proportion. 0.5 and 12 are the means of the proportion.

$4:6 = 6:9$

6 is the geometric mean of 4 and 9.

$a:b = c:d$ can also be written as $\dfrac{a}{b} = \dfrac{c}{d}$. We can multiply both sides of $\dfrac{a}{b} = \dfrac{c}{d}$ by bd to show that $ad = bc$. Likewise, we can divide both sides of $ad = bc$ by bd to get $\dfrac{a}{b} = \dfrac{c}{d}$.

But note that a, b, c and d cannot be zero.

Given that $\dfrac{8}{10} = \dfrac{12}{15}$, multiplying both sides by 10×15 gives $15 \times 8 = 12 \times 10$. Given that $15 \times 8 = 12 \times 10$, dividing both sides by 10×15 gives $\dfrac{8}{10} = \dfrac{12}{15}$.

Summary

The basic properties of proportion

If $a:b = c:d$ or $\dfrac{a}{b} = \dfrac{c}{d}$, $ad = bc$. In turn, if a, b, c and d are not zero and $ad = bc$, then $a:b = c:d$ or $\dfrac{a}{b} = \dfrac{c}{d}$.

Example 1 Find the value of x in each equation.

a. $x:4.8 = 5:2$

b. $4:x = 1\frac{1}{2}:1$

c. $\frac{x}{20} = \frac{11}{4}$

d. $15:x = 1.2:1.5$

Solution

a. Since $x:4.8 = 5:2$, $2x = 5 \times 4.8$, then $x = 24 \div 2 = 12$

b. Since $4:x = 1\frac{1}{2}:1$, $1\frac{1}{2}x = 4$, $x = 4 \div 1\frac{1}{2}$

Then $x = 4 \div \frac{3}{2}$, $x = 4 \times \frac{2}{3} = \frac{8}{3}$

c. Since $\frac{x}{20} = \frac{11}{4}$, $4x = 11 \times 20$, $x = \frac{11 \times 20}{4}$. $x = 55$

d. Since $15:x = 1.2:1.5$, $1.2x = 15 \times 1.5$, $x = \frac{15 \times 15}{12}$. $x = \frac{75}{4}$

Example 2 Six kilograms of blueberries cost £100. The manager of the smoothie shop has £250. How many kilograms of blueberries can she buy?

Solution

Method 1: One kilogram of blueberries costs £$\frac{100}{6}$ = £$\frac{50}{3}$.

With £250 the amount of blueberries the manager can buy is

$250 \div \frac{50}{3} = 250 \times \frac{3}{50} = 15$ kg.

Method 2: Assume that the manager can buy x kilograms of blueberries with £250.

Quantity of blueberries (kg)	Price (£)
6	100
x	250

How can we work that out?

From the relationship between the price of blueberries and the quantity of blueberries, we know that

$\frac{6}{100} = \frac{x}{250}$

$100x = 250 \times 6$

$x = \frac{250 \times 6}{100}$, $x = 15$

We can also use the equation: $\frac{x}{6} = \frac{250}{100}$

The manager can buy 15 kilograms of blueberries with £250.

Practice 3.3

1. **Find the value of x in each equation.**

   a. $x : 1\frac{1}{5} = 6\frac{1}{4} : 2$

   b. $6 : x = 2\frac{2}{5} : 1$

   c. $\dfrac{60}{x} = \dfrac{2}{5}$

2. **Use proportion to answer these questions.**

   a. The height of a pile of 12 books, all of the same thickness, is 30 centimetres. What is the height of a pile of 20 books of the same thickness?

   b. It costs Alex £10 to buy 12 notebooks. How much money does he need to buy 27 of these notebooks?

Section Two: Percentages
3.4 The meaning of percentages
Think!

Many areas of the world are hit by sandstorms in varying degrees. Planting trees and extensive areas of vegetation is one of the methods used to prevent and control sandstorms. This table lists the number of different species of tree in one area. Which species is the best to plant?

Species	Number of trees planted	Number of living trees	Ratio of the number of living trees to the total number planted
A	20	17	$\frac{17}{20}$
B	25	23	$\frac{23}{25}$
C	50	42	$\frac{42}{50}$
D	10	8	$\frac{8}{10}$

It is not easy to see which species of tree is best to plant from the table. It would be easier to decide if the ratios were expressed as the number of living trees to every 100 trees planted.

$$\frac{17}{20} = \frac{17 \times 5}{20 \times 5} = \frac{85}{100}$$

$$\frac{23}{25} = \frac{23 \times 4}{25 \times 4} = \frac{92}{100}$$

$$\frac{42}{50} = \frac{42 \times 2}{50 \times 2} = \frac{84}{100}$$

$$\frac{8}{10} = \frac{8 \times 10}{10 \times 10} = \frac{80}{100}$$

Because $\frac{92}{100} > \frac{85}{100} > \frac{84}{100} > \frac{80}{100}$, it is best to plant trees of species B.

In the last example, the ratio for species A of the number of living trees to the total number planted is represented as $\frac{17}{20}$, which can be expressed as $\frac{85}{100}$. This means that there are 85 living trees of species A for every 100 that were planted. So if the number planted is 100 per cent, the number of living trees is eighty-five per cent.

> The ratio of two numbers $\frac{n}{100}$ can be expressed as a **percentage** written as $n\%$, which is read as 'n per cent'. The symbol % is a percentage sign and is read as 'per cent'.

For example, 42% is $\frac{42}{100}$, read as forty-two per cent; 125% is $\frac{125}{100}$, read as one hundred and twenty-five per cent.

Think!

What fraction of the total shape is shaded in each of the diagrams? Work it out in terms of percentages.

Since a percentage is a special fraction, with 100 as the denominator, it is easy to understand the relationship between the part and the whole. This makes it convenient for making comparisons, so it is widely used in industrial and agricultural production systems, as well as in everyday life. For example, over a period of 20 years, the amount of urban green space in Shanghai increased significantly. Expressed as a percentage, the amount of open green space increased from 12.4% in 1990 to 38.2% in 2010.

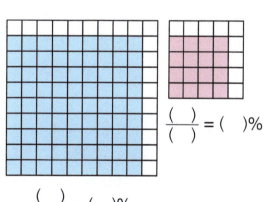

$\frac{(\quad)}{(\quad)} = (\quad)\%$

$\frac{(\quad)}{(\quad)} = (\quad)\%$

Example 1

Convert these percentages into fractions in their simplest form.

a. 62%   **b.** 55%   **c.** 37.5%   **d.** 125%

Solution

a. $62\% = \dfrac{62}{100} = \dfrac{31}{50}$

b. $55\% = \dfrac{55}{100} = \dfrac{11}{20}$

c. $37.5\% = 37.5 \div 100 = \dfrac{375}{1000} = \dfrac{3}{8}$

d. $125\% = \dfrac{125}{100} = \dfrac{5}{4}$

The result of $30 \div 40$ can be represented as

$$\dfrac{30}{40} = \dfrac{3}{4} = 0.75 = 75\%$$

In everyday life, you will see different representations for different situations. For example, if Dylan spent £30 on 40 kiwi fruits, the price of one kiwi fruit could be written as £0.75. As another example, suppose that among 40 pupils in a class there are 30 pupils who love maths. This could be written as 75% or $\dfrac{3}{4}$. Therefore, it is very important to be able to work with percentages, fractions and decimals and convert between them.

Example 2 Convert these decimals to percentages.

a. 0.47   **b.** 0.028

c. 2.73   **d.** 0.3

Solution

a. $0.47 = 0.47 \times 100\% = 47\%$

b. $0.028 = 0.028 \times 100\% = 2.8\%$

c. $2.73 = 2.73 \times 100\% = 273\%$

d. $0.3 = 0.3 \times 100\% = 30\%$

> To turn a decimal into a percentage, move the decimal point two places to the right and write the percentage sign at the end.
>
> $0.47 \to 47\%$ $0.028 \to 2.8\%$
> $2.73 \to 273\%$ $0.3 \to 30\%$

Example 3 Convert each percentage to a decimal or an integer.

a. 40.2%   **b.** 125.2%

c. 0.52%   **d.** 200%

Solution

a. $40.2\% = 40.2 \div 100 = \dfrac{402}{1000} = 0.402$

b. $125.2\% = 125.2 \div 100 = \dfrac{1252}{1000} = 1.252$

c. $0.52\% = 0.52 \div 100 = \dfrac{52}{10\,000} = 0.0052$

d. $200\% = \dfrac{200}{100} = 2$

> To turn a percentage into a decimal, move the decimal point two places to the left and drop the percentage sign.
>
> $40.2\% \to 0.402$
> $125.2\% \to 1.252$
> $0.52\% \to 0.0052$
> $200\% \to 2$

Example 4 Convert these fractions into decimals, then into percentages.

a. $\dfrac{1}{4}$ b. $\dfrac{5}{8}$ c. $\dfrac{5}{6}$ d. $\dfrac{7}{5}$

Solution

a. $\dfrac{1}{4} = 0.25 = 25\%$

b. $\dfrac{5}{8} = 0.625 = 62.5\%$

c. $\dfrac{5}{6} \approx 0.833 = 83.3\%$

d. $\dfrac{7}{5} = 1.4 = 140\%$

We can also do it like this:
$$\dfrac{1}{4} = \dfrac{1 \times 25}{4 \times 25} = \dfrac{25}{100}$$

To convert a fraction into a percentage, convert the fraction to a decimal, and then convert the decimal to a percentage.

*Practice 3.4

1. Read these numbers to a partner.

35%, 100%, 180%, 0.4%

2. Use the % symbol to represent these percentages.

Thirty per cent, one hundred and twenty per cent, one point five per cent.

3. Convert these numbers to percentages.

a. 0.2   b. 0.05   c. $\dfrac{1}{10}$ d. $\dfrac{28}{70}$ e. $1\dfrac{3}{4}$

4. Convert these percentages to decimal numbers or whole numbers.

a. 3%   b. 80%   c. 1.25%   d. 120%   e. 300%

5. Convert these percentages to fractions in their simplest form.

0.1%, 20%, 16%, 12.5%, 135%, 10.23%

6. Find the quotients. Then, convert the quotients into percentages.

a. $240 \div 600$ b. $6 \div 9.6$ c. $144 \div 120$ d. $12.5 \div 50$

*In this exercise, unless the question specifies the accuracy, give the quotients correct to 3 decimal places.

3.5 Applications of percentages

Example 1 In China there are around 30 000 different plant species, and of these around 17 300 are native Chinese species. Work out the percentage of the total number of plant species in China that represents native Chinese species. (Give the percentage to 1 decimal place.)

Analysis You need to express the total number of native Chinese species as a percentage of the total number of plant species in China.

Solution $17\,300 \div 30\,000 = \dfrac{17\,300}{30\,000} = \dfrac{173}{300} = 57.7\%$

Of the plants that grow in China, 57.7% are native species.

Percentages are commonly used in business and education.

Pass rate $= \dfrac{\text{number passing the test}}{\text{number taking the test}} \times 100\%$

Quality control rate $= \dfrac{\text{number of goods passing quality criteria}}{\text{number of goods tested}} \times 100\%$

Rate of growth $= \dfrac{\text{increase in output or production}}{\text{original output or production}} \times 100\%$

Attendance rate $= \dfrac{\text{number actually attending}}{\text{number that should be attending}} \times 100\%$ and so on.

Example 2

On 3 December 2002, the International Exhibition Bureau held its 132nd meeting in Monaco, to choose the host city for the 2010 World Expo. In the final round of voting, a total of 88 members attended the vote. Shanghai, China won 54 votes and became the host city of Expo 2010. What percentage of voters chose Shanghai in this round of voting? (Give the percentage correct to 1 decimal place.)

Analysis

Percentage of the vote $= \dfrac{\text{number of votes won}}{\text{number of votes cast}} \times 100\%$

Solution

The vote = $\dfrac{54}{88} \approx 0.614 = 61.4\%$

The vote in this round of voting was 61.4%.

Example 3

A car parts factory produces 1000 parts per day. Of these 1000 products, 25 are defective. Evaluate the quality assessment rate for these products.

Solution

Percentage passing = $\dfrac{1000 - 25}{1000} = \dfrac{975}{1000} = 0.975 = 97.5\%$

The quality assessment rate for these products is 97.5%.

Example 4

Controlling the discharge of pollutants from factories, and limiting their concentration, is an important environmental protection measure. According to available statistics, in nearly 3000 boiler inspections in 82 key cities, 72.7% of boiler smoke dust removal measures had reached the required standard for environmental protection. How many boilers passed the test for removal of smoke and dust?

Solution

3000 × 72.7% = 2181 (boilers)
So 2181 boilers passed the test for removal of smoke and dust.

 # Think!

What information can you find out from this passage?

The city's total industrial output in the second quarter of this year was £100 billion, up 6.2% from the first quarter, and is expected to increase by a percentage point in the third quarter from the second quarter.

What is the growth rate?	What does it mean to raise one percentage point?	Can we find the industrial output value for the third quarter?

Growth rate = $\dfrac{\text{growth in number}}{\text{original number}} \times 100\%$

1 percentage point is the equivalent of 1%. This may show a percentage increase or decrease. Here the growth rate in the third quarter will be 6.2% + 1% = 7.2%.

$7.2\% = \dfrac{\text{industrial output in 3rd quarter} - \text{industrial output in 2nd quarter}}{\text{industrial output in 2nd quarter}} \times 100\%$

Set the industrial output in the third quarter as £x billion, then we can say:

$\dfrac{x - 100}{100} = 7.2\%$,

so $x = 100 + 100 \times 7.2\%$, $x = 107.2$

> It can be solved by listing the equation 100(1 + 7.2%) directly.

So the industrial output in the third quarter is expected to be £107.2 billion.

Think!

Industrial output in the third quarter increases by 1% based on an output of £100 billion in the second quarter, but compared with the third quarter's industrial output the industrial output in the fourth quarter decreases by 1%. Can industrial output in the fourth quarter be £100 billion or not?

> What does dropping a percentage point mean?

Practice 3.5 (1)

1. **There are 48 pupils in Year 6 Class 2. In a maths test, 45 pupils passed and 10 of them passed with distinction. What percentage of the class passed with distinction? What percentage achieved the basic pass level?**

2. **40 kg of meat contains 6 kg of protein. What is the percentage of protein in the meat?**

3. **The number of school days in one academic year was 210. Dylan was absent on 14 days. What was his percentage absence rate for the year?**

4. There are 60 pupils in Year 6, and 18 of them wear glasses. What percentage of the pupils in Year 6 don't wear glasses?

5. Last year, the total annual sales at a shopping mall were £2.1 million. This was an increase of 5.6% on the sales in the previous year. The annual marketing sales plan for next year calls for a growth rate equivalent to an increase of one per cent over the previous year. What must the sales for next year be to meet the target of the annual sales plan?

Example 5
A statistics question

The diagram shows the results of a survey of how 228 pupils come to school.

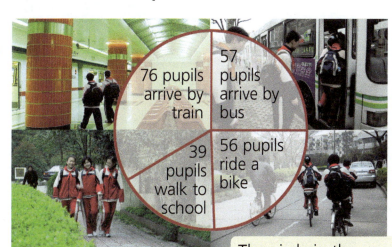

76 pupils arrive by train

57 pupils arrive by bus

39 pupils walk to school

56 pupils ride a bike

a. What percentage of pupils take the bus?

b. What percentage of pupils take the train?

c. What percentage of pupils walk to school?

d. What percentage of pupils ride a bike to school?

The circle in the diagram is a **pie chart**. Each part represents a group of pupils.

Solution

a. The percentage of pupils travelling to school by bus is

$$\frac{57}{228} = 0.25 = 25\%$$

 b. The percentage of pupils travelling to school by train is

$$\frac{76}{228} \approx 0.333 = 33.3\%$$

c. The percentage of pupils walking to school is

$$\frac{39}{228} \approx 0.171 = 17.1\%$$

d. The percentage of pupils riding a bike to school is $\frac{56}{228} \approx 0.246 = 24.6\%$

We can also say
100% − 25% − 33.3% − 17.1%
= 24.6%

The percentages of pupils travelling to school by bus, by train, walking and riding a bike are 25%, 33.3%, 17.1% and 24.6% respectively.

Example 6 A statistics question

The bar chart shows the test marks of Year 6 pupils in Rutherford School. Given that the total number of pupils in this year is 308, use the data in the chart to find the percentage of pupils who gained 81–85 marks, 86–90 marks and 91–95 marks respectively.

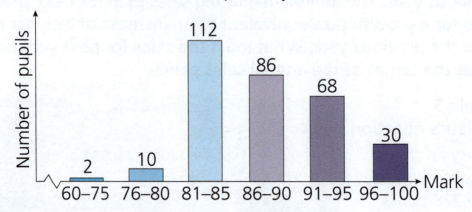

Solution

The total number of pupils in the year is 308.

The number of pupils who gained 81–85 marks is 112.

The number of pupils who gained 86–90 marks is 86.

The number of pupils who gained 91–95 marks is 68.

 So, the percentage of pupils who gained 81–85 marks is

$\frac{112}{308} \times 100\% \approx 36.4\%$

The percentage of pupils who gained 86–90 marks is

$\frac{86}{308} \times 100\% \approx 27.9\%$

The percentage of pupils who gained 91–95 marks is

$\frac{68}{308} \times 100\% \approx 22.1\%$

The percentages of pupils who gained 81–85 marks, 86–90 marks and 91–95 marks in the test are 36.4%, 27.9% and 22.1% respectively.

Practice 3.5 (2)

1. Fill in the missing percentage.

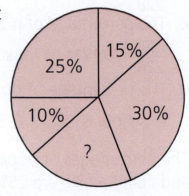

2. Look at the diagram and answer the questions.

a. What percentage of all human diseases are genetic diseases?

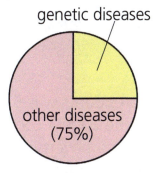

genetic diseases

other diseases (75%)

b. What percentage of the global population are people with genetic diseases?

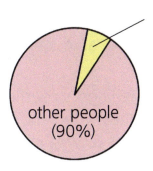

people with genetic diseases

other people (90%)

3. Carry out a survey among the pupils in your class. Find out about the TV programmes they watch in a week and then fill in the table.

	News programmes	Cartoons	Dramas and soaps
Number of pupils			
Percentage of total class			

Example 7 The problem of Engel's coefficient

Economists call the ratio of household or individual expenditure on food consumption to total consumption expenditure **Engel's coefficient**.

$$\text{Engel's coefficient} = \frac{\text{expenditure on food}}{\text{total expenditure}} \times 100\%$$

Engel's coefficient can be used to describe different types of consumption, but can also indirectly show the different stages of development of a country. The requirements of the Food and Agriculture Organization of the United Nations are listed in this table.

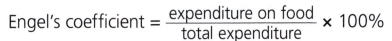

Engel's coefficient is				
≥ 60%	50–60%	40–50%	30%–40%	< 30%
Absolute poverty	Adequately fed and clothed	Comparatively well-off	Well-off	Richest

Note: 50–60% includes all data above and including 50% and up to but not including 60%, and so on.

Referring to the tables for Engel's coefficient and for urban and rural residents for China, calculate the stage for each of these years.

		Year		
		1978	1995	2016
Engel's coefficient	Urban residents	57.5%	49%	31.4%
	Rural residents	67.7%	58.6%	32.2%

Solution

In China in 1978 the Engel's coefficient of urban residents was 57.5%, indicating the adequately fed and clothed stage; the Engel's coefficient for rural residents was 67.7%, indicating the absolute poverty stage.

In 1995 the Engel's coefficient of urban residents was 49%, indicating the comparatively well-off stage; the Engel's coefficient of rural residents was 58.6%, indicating the adequately fed and clothed stage.

By 2016 the Engel's coefficient of urban residents had dropped to 31.4%, indicating the well-off stage; the Engel's coefficient of rural residents was 32.2%, also indicating the well-off stage.

Example 8 A profit and loss problem

A shop bought 100 suits at a cost price of £200 each and sold them for £280 each. They bought 100 pairs of leather shoes at a cost price of £300 per pair and sold them for £390 per pair, as shown in the table.

	Cost price (£)	Selling price (£)	Profit (£)
Suits	200	280	280 − 200 = 80
Leather shoes	300	390	390 − 300 = 90

Was the profit margin greater for suits or for leather shoes?

Analysis

$$\text{Percentage profit} = \frac{\text{profit}}{\text{cost price}} \times 100\% = \frac{\text{selling price} - \text{cost price}}{\text{cost price}} \times 100\%$$

In the above question, you only need to compare the profitability of one suit and one pair of shoes.

Solution The profitability of selling one suit $= \dfrac{280 - 200}{200} = 40\%$

The profitability of selling one pair of leather shoes $= \dfrac{390 - 300}{300} = 30\%$

The profit margin was greater for selling suits.

As well as profitability, there can be a loss rate.

$$\text{Percentage loss} = \frac{\text{loss}}{\text{cost price}} \times 100\% = \frac{\text{cost price} - \text{selling price}}{\text{cost price}} \times 100\%$$

Example 9 A profit and loss problem

The cost price of a computer is £4000. The shop sells it to a customer at a profit of 30%. What is the selling price?

Solution

Method 1: Profit = cost × profitability,
so profit = 4000 × 30% = £1200
and profit = cost price − selling price
so selling price = cost price + profit = 4000 + 1200 = £5200

Method 2: Selling price = 4000 × (1 + 30%)
= 4000 × 1.3
= 5200
The selling price of this computer is £5200.

Shops often have sales with discounted prices, for example:

The original price of a commodity is £100. In a sale offering 20% off the original price, the actual price of the commodity is £100 × 80% = £80.

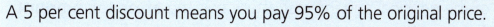

A 5 per cent discount means you pay 95% of the original price.
A 20 per cent discount means you pay 80% of the original price.
A 50 per cent discount means you pay 50% of the original price.

The original price of a jacket was £480 but it is sold at a reduction of £120. What is the percentage discount?

A TV is sold with a 20 per cent discount. The sale price is £1600. What was the original price?

Can you help Emma and Dylan answer these two questions?

Practice 3.5 (3)

1. **The cost price of a dress is £80. If it is sold with a 20% profit, what is the selling price?**

2. **At the start of a new term, the local bookshop shares some of its profits with the pupils, by offering them a discount of 20% on books. Dylan buys a set of books with an original price of £60. What does he pay?**

3. **A computer is sold with 15% off the original price. The sale price is £5100. What was the original price of this computer?**

4. **The price of a sports outfit was £380.**

   a. **What is the percentage discount if the price is reduced by £152?**

   b. **What is the percentage discount if the price is reduced to £152?**

You can earn **interest** if you deposit money in a bank. You must pay interest if you borrow money from the bank. This is called taking out a **loan**. The amount of money you deposit or borrow is called the **principal**. The interest is calculated as a percentage of the principal, called the **interest rate**. If interest is paid every month, this percentage is the **monthly interest rate**; if interest is paid once a year, the percentage is the **annual interest rate**.

In some countries, if people deposit money into a bank to earn interest, they must pay tax, for example, at a rate of 20% of the interest earned.

The sum of the principal and interest after tax is the **after-tax amount** or the **net amount**.

For example, if you deposit £100 into a bank at an annual interest rate of 2%, then you will earn interest of £2 per year. The tax on the interest that will be deducted is 2 × 20% = £0.40, the net amount after tax (principal and taxed interest) is £(100 + 2 − 0.40) = £101.60.

> The interest we are looking at here is called **simple interest**. In everyday life, businesses use **compound interest**, which you will learn about in the future.

Example 10 A profit and tax question

Emma's mum deposits £1500 into a bank offering a monthly interest rate of 0.11%. After a full year, she pays 20% tax on the interest. How much after-tax interest can Emma's mum get at the end of the year?

Solution

The interest for a full year

= 1500 × 0.11% × 12

= £19.80

The tax paid on the interest

= 19.8 × 20%

= £3.96

The net interest Emma's mum gets after tax

= 19.80 − 3.96

= £15.84

After a year, Emma's mum gets £15.84 net interest.

How can we convert the monthly interest rate to the annual interest rate?

We write the formula as:

> Interest = principal × interest rate × the length of time

Example 11 A profit and tax question

Mr Roberts borrows £120 000 from a bank, at an annual interest rate of 4.5% simple interest, for 5 years. How much interest will he pay over the 5 years (at maturity)?

Solution   Interest = principal × interest rate × length of time

= 120 000 × 4.5% × 5

= £27 000

Mr Roberts should pay £27 000 interest at maturity.

Practice 3.5 (4)

1. Alex deposits £2000 into a bank for a year. The monthly interest rate is 0.14%, and he should pay tax on the interest at 20%. How much interest does Alex actually get?

2. Emma's dad takes out a policy with an insurance company. His insured amount is £10000. The annual rate of return is 5%, and it will be paid to the insured every three years. How much money can Emma's dad expect three years later?

3. A company made a profit of £2050000 last year. Tax must be paid at the rate of 33%. How much tax did the company pay last year? (Give your answer correct to the nearest £10000.)

4. Set up a small bank in your class or group. Role play savings activities at a suitable bank rate.

3.6 Equally likely outcomes

What do you remember about **probability**? If you watch the daily weather forecast on TV, you may hear the weather forecaster say, 'The probability of rain tomorrow is 80%…' This means that there is an 80% chance of rain tomorrow, although it may not rain.

Try it out!

The disc in the diagram is divided into 8 equal parts and the pointer spins around the centre. What is the probability that the pointer will stop inside the region marked 2?

Think!

The eight regions numbered 1, 2, 3, 4, 5, 6, 7 and 8 are all exactly the same shape and size. The probability of the pointer stopping in any of these eight regions is the same, and stopping within area 2 is only one of the eight possible choices. Therefore the probability that the pointer falls within any region is $\frac{1}{8}$.

The capital letter P is used to represent the probability. The probability that the pointer falls within region 2 is $P(2) = \frac{1}{8}$ which can also be written as a percentage, 12.5%.

The pointer rotates around the centre of the disc. The pointer stopping within a region on the disc is called an **event**. There are, in total, 8 possible **outcomes** of this event. The probabilities of all these outcomes are equal, so the probability of the pointer stopping in any one of them is $\frac{1}{8}$.

Summary

$$P = \frac{\text{number of ways this event can happen}}{\text{total number of possible outcomes}}$$

P is the first letter of the word **probability**, so it is used to represent probability.

Example 1

The disc in the diagram is divided into seven regions, of which three are coloured red, three are blue and one is white. The pointer spins around the centre. Find the probability of the pointer stopping in a red region.

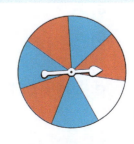

Solution

The pointer rotates around the centre, the total number of possible outcomes (the regions on the disc) is 7. There are 3 red regions, so the probability of the spinner stopping in a red region is $P(3) = \frac{3}{7}$.

We could also say that the red regions account for $\frac{3}{7}$ of the entire circle, so the probability that the pointer will stop in a red region is $\frac{3}{7}$.

← Is the probability of the pointer stopping within the blue area equal to the probability of the pointer stopping within the red area?

Example 2

If you pick a card from a normal pack of 52 playing cards there are in total 52 equally likely outcomes.

a. List all possible ways of picking a king.

b. Find the probability of picking the king of hearts.

c. Find the probability of picking up a king.

Solution

a. There are four kings in the pack: king of hearts, king of spades, king of diamonds, king of clubs.

b. $P(K\heartsuit) = \frac{1}{52}$

Or you can say the probability of picking the king of hearts is about 1.9%.

← $\frac{1}{52} \approx 0.019 = 1.9\%$

c. $P(K) = \frac{4}{52} = \frac{1}{13}$

Or you can say the probability of picking a king is 7.7%.

← $\frac{1}{13} \approx 0.077 = 7.7\%$

 ## Practice 3.6

1. This disc is divided into 12 equal parts, lettered A–L. Find the probability of the pointer stopping on these regions.

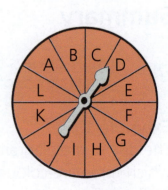

   a. A

   b. B

   c. C or D

   d. E or F or K

2. Roll a dice. Find the probability of scoring 1.

3. There are two identical discs. One is divided into 6 equal regions, the other is divided into 4 equal regions. The regions are lettered and numbered, as shown.

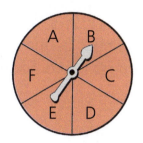 

  a. Write all the possible outcomes from the two spinners, in the form 'letter–number', for example, A–1, A–2.

  b. Find the probability of each of these outcomes.
     i) A–1   ii) C–3   iii) F–odd number

Unit summary

After working through this unit, you now understand important concepts and properties of ratio and percentage, and the relationship between percentages and decimals. You have gained some basic understanding and simple applications of percentages in real life and started to study probabilities of equally likely outcomes and to use percentages to answer problems.

The framework of this unit is as shown below.

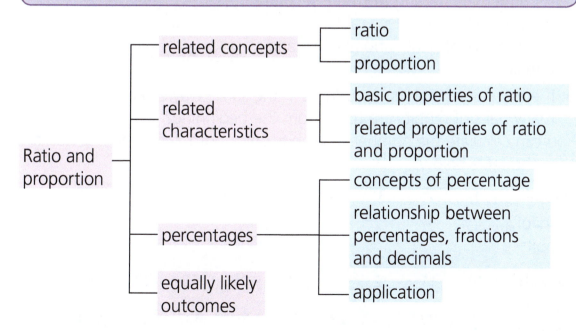

📖 Extra reading material: Looking for a pattern

Consider the numbers 1, 2, 3, 4, ..., 100. Taking the numbers two at a time, divide each number by the previous one. You need to use your calculator after the first few divisions. Write the ratio for each pair:

$$\frac{2}{1} = 2, \frac{3}{2} = 1.5, \frac{4}{3} = 1.3, \frac{5}{4} = 1.25, \ldots$$

$$\frac{99}{98} \approx 1.010\,204\,082, \frac{100}{99} \approx 1.010\,101\,01$$

Looking at the trend of these ratios, you can see that these results are getting closer to the number 1.

Now repeat the activity, but this time just use the odd numbers 1, 3, 5, 7, ..., 1001, 1003, ... following the previous method and using a calculator. Write the ratio values and look for a trend. What conclusion can you make?

Fibonacci (1175–1250) was an Italian mathematician in the Middle Ages. In the year 1202 CE, he wrote *The Abacus Book*. In this book there is a puzzle.

a. Assume that one-month-old rabbits (male and female) are not yet mature, so they can't breed, but at the age of two months they are mature.

Assume that, starting from the second month, each month two rabbits breed a pair of baby rabbits (male and female).

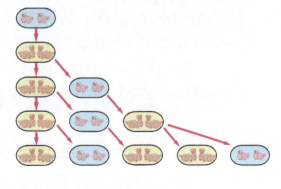

b. If every pair of rabbits reproduces in the same way as above, how many pairs of rabbits are there from the beginning?

You can calculate the number of rabbits per month, from the beginning, as in the table below.

Month	1	2	3	4	5	6	7	8	9
Pairs of rabbits	1	1	2	3	5	8	13	21	34

Month	10	11	12	13	14	15	16	17	18
Pairs of rabbits	55	89	144	233	377	610	987	1597	2584

From the table, you can draw up these rules.

- From the third month, the number of pairs of rabbits is equal to the sum of the pairs for the previous two months.

- If you divide the number of rabbits in one month by the number of rabbits in the following month, the result approaches a constant ratio. For example, there is one pair of rabbits in the second month, two pairs of rabbits in the third month, then

$$\frac{\text{the number of pairs of rabbits in the second month}}{\text{the number of pairs of rabbits in the third month}} = \frac{1}{2} = 0.5.$$

Eventually, you find:

$$\frac{\text{the number of pairs of rabbits in the eighth month}}{\text{the number of pairs of rabbits in the ninth month}} = \frac{21}{34} \approx 0.617\,647\,058.$$

Using a calculator, carefully work out the results of each of the ratio values in the table, then observe and summarise the trend of these results. All ratio values get very close to a constant. Can you estimate what this constant number will be? (Give your answer to 3 decimal places.)

🔭 Investigation activity: Applying percentages

You know that everything on Earth depends on the Sun, air and water. Water is precious, but the world's water is not all fresh water. Fresh water accounts for only 2.5% of all water resources. Of this 2.5%, 99.66% is in the ice caps, glacier water and deep ground water, and only 0.34% is available fresh water. Of this subtotal of 0.34% usable water, fresh water resources in China account for 6% of the world's total.

This diagram shows it more clearly.

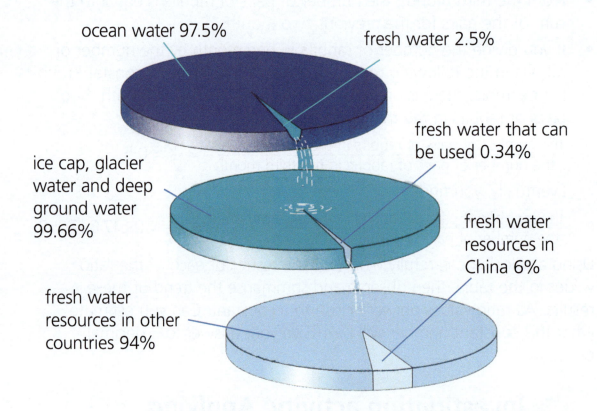

ocean water 97.5%

fresh water 2.5%

fresh water that can be used 0.34%

ice cap, glacier water and deep ground water 99.66%

fresh water resources in China 6%

fresh water resources in other countries 94%

Look at the diagram carefully and read the numbers. What do you think of it? Do you have a deeper understanding of percentages?

? Problems

1. Work out the percentage of the world's fresh water that humans can actually use from the world's water reserves.

2. At the beginning of the 21st century, the world's population was about 6 billion and the population of China was about 1.3 billion. Based on the data given in the diagram, calculate China's fresh water resources per person as a percentage of the world's resources per person.

    According to the statistics, China's fresh water resources are only less than those of Brazil, Russia and Canada, ranking fourth in the world. Some people say that China's fresh water resources are very plentiful. From your calculated results, do you agree with their point of view?

3. Use the internet and other resources to find out more about the world's water resources and any problems relating to them. Write a paragraph, using percentages, to describe what you find.

Unit Four
Circles and sectors

There are many beautiful shapes and structures around us. What special features do they have? How can we study them in mathematics?

What do you observe in these two pictures?

 The path of a moving point forms a curve or a line, and a moving line forms a surface, or a plane.

You will learn more about the properties and features of these shapes in this unit.

Section One: Circumference and arc length

4.1 Circumference

Think!

Two remote-controlled model cars are driven around a square, with a side length of 3 m, and a circle, of diameter 3 m, in a race. If they start off at the same time at the same speed, which will arrive back at the starting point first?

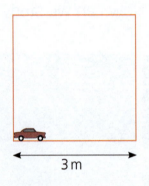

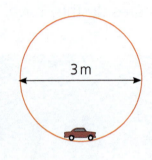

3 m

3 m

We only need to compare the circumference of the circle and the perimeter of the square.

How can we work out the circumference of the circle?

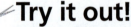

Try it out!

Use £2 and 10p coins for these experiments.

1. First, measure the diameter of each coin.
2. Measure the circumference of each coin.

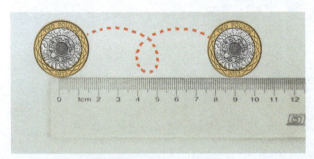

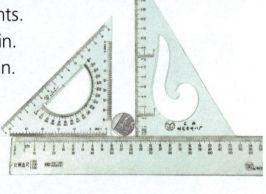

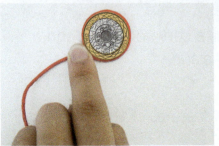

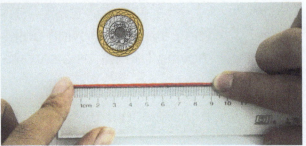

Put your measuring data in this table and calculate the ratio value of C and d. (Round to the nearest hundredth.)

	Diameter d	Circumference C	Ratio value of C and d
£2 coin			
10p coin			

Find some other round objects and repeat your experiments.

Although these circles are different sizes, what relationship between circumference and diameter can you find by measuring and calculating?

From your experiments, measuring and calculations, you should find that the circumference is just over three times the diameter every time. In fact, this number has a fixed value, which is known as the circumference : diameter ratio, and is represented by the Greek letter π. You read this as **pi**.

Circumference ÷ diameter
= circumference : diameter ratio

Over the centuries, people have found that π is an infinite non-recurring decimal and it approximates 3.14, which means π ≈ 3.14.*

Mathematicians have been studying the circumference : diameter ratio for many centuries. Archimedes was working on it in 250 BCE. In about the fifth century CE, Chinese mathematicians, including Zu Chongzhi during the Liu Song and Southern Qi Dynasties, used simple calculation tools, such as pens and rulers, to calculate the ratio to 7 decimal places. This was a great achievement at the time. Pupils who are interested can search the internet to find out more.

Summary

Using C to represent circumference, d to represent diameter and r to represent radius:

$$C = \pi d \quad \text{or} \quad C = 2\pi r$$

Example 1 A royal water lily leaf approximates a circle and its diameter is almost 0.95 metres. What is the circumference of this leaf? (Round your answer to 2 decimal places.)

*In this unit, unless instructed otherwise, take π as 3.14 and round the result of your calculation to the nearest hundredth.

Solution $d = 0.95\,\text{m}$

$C = \pi d = 3.14 \times 0.95 = 2.983 \approx 2.98\,\text{m}$

The circumference of this leaf is $2.98\,\text{m}$.

Example 2

A satellite orbits the Earth and the path of its flight approximates to a circle. The distance from the satellite to the surface of the Earth is $500\,\text{km}$ and it orbits the Earth 14 times. How far does the satellite travel? (Take the radius of the Earth as $6400\,\text{km}$.)

Solution

Radius of the orbit, $R = 500 + 6400 = 6900\,\text{km}$

Circumference of the orbit, $C = 2\pi R = 2 \times 3.14 \times 6900 = 43\,332\,\text{km}$

$14C = 43\,332 \times 14 = 606\,648$

The distance travelled by the satellite around the Earth is $606\,648\,\text{km}$.

Example 3

In the diagram, the circumference of the exterior circle of the ring $C_1 = 250\,\text{cm}$ and the circumference of the inner circle $C_2 = 150\,\text{cm}$.

What is the width, d, of the ring? (Round the result to the nearest $0.1\,\text{cm}$.)

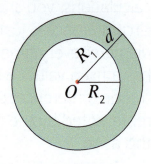

Solution

$C = 2\pi R = 2 \times 3.14 \times R = 6.28 \times R$

$R = C \div 6.28$.

Let the radius of the exterior circle be R_1 and the radius of the inner circle be R_2.

Then $R_1 = C_1 \div 6.28$, $R_2 = C_2 \div 6.28$,

$d = R_1 - R_2 = (C_1 - C_2) \div 6.28$

$= (250 - 150) \div 6.28$

≈ 15.9

The width, d, of the ring is $15.9\,\text{cm}$.

Practice 4.1

1. Calculate the circumference of each circle. (units: cm)

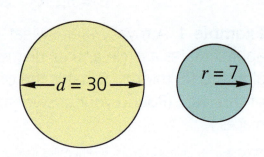

2. What is the perimeter of a semicircle of diameter 5 cm? Who has calculated accurately, Dylan, Poppy or Emma? Why?

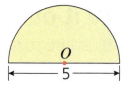

| 3.14 × 5 + 5 | 3.14 × 5 ÷ 2 | 3.14 × 5 ÷ 2 + 5 |

3. A dairy farmer plans to use thick wire to put up a circular fence of radius 120 m (as shown in the picture). If the farmer plans to use three strands of wire for the fence, what length of wire does he need to buy?

4. Calculate the perimeter of the track. (units: m)

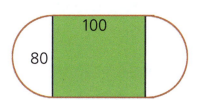

4.2 Arc length

The diagram on the left is a three-colour spinner, consisting of three different coloured discs. Use the template at the back of this book to make three discs. Slide the discs together along the slits and then rotate each disc until the colours are evenly spaced, and then spin the spinner. If you change the proportion of the exposed parts of the three discs, you should see different colours when you spin it. You should be able to make seven different colours: red, orange, yellow, green, blue, purple and white.

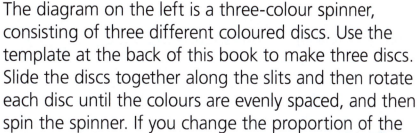

In the diagram on the right, the section of the circle marked in red between the two points A and B is an arc. You write this as $\overarc{AB}$ and you read it as 'arc AB'. $\angle AOB$ is called the **central angle** for the arc.

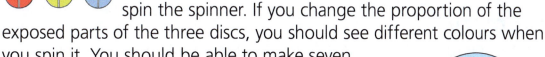

In the same circle, if the central angle of the arc gets bigger, the corresponding arc length gets longer.

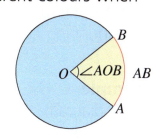

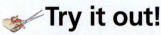
Try it out!

Adjust the spinner and observe the variation of the arc length and the corresponding central angle.

Think!

1. What size is the central angle *AOB*? How much of the circumference is taken up by the arc length for each different angle *AOB*?

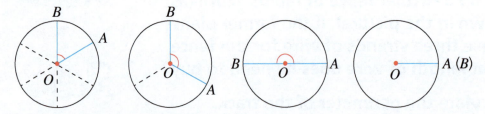

2. How does the central angle *n* affect the corresponding arc length on the circumference?

Circumference $C = 2\pi r$, the corresponding central angle is 360°.

> A central angle of 1° corresponds to an arc
> length $= \dfrac{1}{360} \times 2\pi r = \dfrac{1}{180} \times \pi r$
> A central angle of *n*° corresponds to an arc
> length $= \dfrac{n}{360} \times 2\pi r = \dfrac{n}{180} \times \pi r$

Summary

Suppose the radius of the circle is *r*, the central angle is *n*° and the corresponding arc length is *l*. Then:

$$l = \frac{n}{180}\,\pi r$$

Example

In the diagram, the lengths of the three sides of triangle *ABC* are all 27 mm. Take *A*, *B* and *C*, in turn, as the centre of a circle and draw arcs of radius 27 mm. Calculate the sum of the three arc lengths.

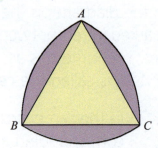

Solution

The central angle for $\widehat{AC}$, $\widehat{AB}$ and $\widehat{BC}$ is 60° in each case.

From the formula for arc length:

$$l = \frac{n}{180}\pi r = \frac{60}{180} \times 3.14 \times 27 = 28.26$$

$3l = 3 \times 28.26 = 84.78$ (mm)

The sum of the three arc lengths is 84.78 mm.

Practice 4.2

1. **Write the missing diagram numbers in the spaces.**
   The central angle is shown in diagrams _____.
   Diagrams _____ do not show the central angle.

   a.

   b.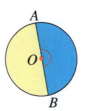

   c.

   d.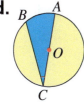

   e.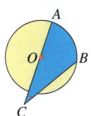

   f.

2. **If the radius, r, of a circle is 1 cm and the central angle is 180°, then the corresponding arc length $l =$ _____ cm.**

3. **If the radius, r, of a circle is 46 cm and the central angle is 18°, then the corresponding arc length $l =$ _____ cm.**

4. **The radius of a circle is 5 cm and the arc length of a part of the circle is 6.28 cm. What is the size of the central angle? (Take π as 3.14.)**

Section Two: Areas of circles and sectors

4.3 Area of a circle

💡 Think!

Dylan tethers his goat to a post on the grass.
What area can the goat reach?

The maximum area that the goat can reach is the area of the circle with the radius equal to the length of the string.

What is the area of the circle?

The size of the region inside the circle is called the **area** of a circle.

You have learned the formulas for the areas of plane shapes such as triangles, parallelograms and trapeziums from earlier years, and you can work them out based on the area of a rectangle. So how can you calculate the area of a curved shape, such as a circle?

✂️ Try it out!

Cut a circle out of card and try to transform it roughly into a linear shape.

Using the methods in this diagram, divide the circle into a number of equal parts, and try to fit the parts closely together.

You should find that the more parts you cut, the closer the shape comes to being a rectangle, and the area of the rectangle comes closer to that of the circle.

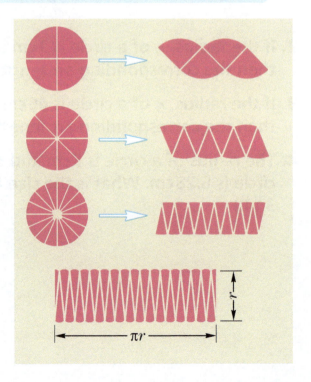

Summary

Let the radius of the circle be r and the area be A.

Area of circle $A = \pi r \times r = \pi r^2$

Example 1

The diameter of a circle is 24 cm. Calculate the area of the circle.

Solution

$r = \dfrac{24}{2} = 12$

$A = \pi r^2 = 3.14 \times 12^2 = 452.16$

The area of this circle is 452.16 cm².

Think!

Dylan's family have a new circular table in their house. His mum asks him to calculate the area of the top of the new table. Can you help Dylan to work it out?

Have a go! You can only calculate the area of the circular table if you measure its circumference or radius first.

Practice 4.3 (1)

1. **True or false?**
   a. The length of the radius of a circle is enlarged 3 times, so the area is enlarged by a factor of 3.   ( )
   b. The circumference of a circle with radius 2 cm is the same as its area.   ( )

2. **Cut a square with side of length 20 cm from card. Cut out the largest circle that you can from it. Find the area of the circle.**

3. **Find the area of a circle with circumference 62.8 m.**

Example 2

The radius of a big wheel in an amusement park is about 50 m. What is the area swept out by a gondola in one rotation? What is the distance travelled by the gondola in one rotation?

Solution

$r = 50$

$A = \pi r^2 = 3.14 \times 50^2 = 3.14 \times 2500$
$\quad = 7850$

$C = 2\pi r = 2 \times 3.14 \times 50 = 314$

The area of rotation is 7850 m² and the length of one rotation is 314 m.

Example 3

A worker is painting the rim of a circular pipe. Its cross-section is shown in the diagram. The outer diameter is 42 cm and the internal diameter is 38 cm. What is the area of the region to be painted?

Analysis

The area of a ring is the difference in the areas of the outer and inner circles.

Solution

Let the radius of the outer circle be R and the radius of the inner circle be r.

$R = \dfrac{42}{2} = 21, r = \dfrac{38}{2} = 19,$

$A = \pi R^2 - \pi r^2$
$\quad = 3.14 \times (21^2 - 19^2)$
$\quad = 3.14 \times 80$
$\quad = 251.2$

The area to be painted is 251.2 cm².

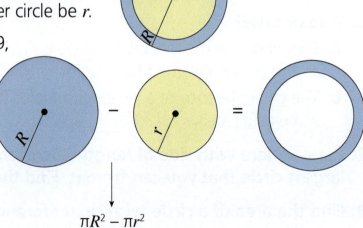

$\pi R^2 - \pi r^2$

Practice 4.3 (2)

1. Multiple choice

  a. The radius of a large circle is twice as long as the radius of a small circle, so the area of the large circle is ( ) as big as the area of the small circle.

    A. twice   **B.** three times   **C.** four times   **D.** five times

  b. The radius of the semicircle in the diagram is r so its area is ( ).

    A. $2\pi r$ **B.** πr^2

    C. $2\pi r^2$ **D.** $\frac{1}{2}\pi r^2$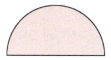

  c. If the area of a circle is enlarged by a factor of 9, the radius is enlarged by a factor of ( ).

    A. 4.5   **B.** 81   **C.** 3   **D.** 18

2. In the picture, the greatest distance that the rotary irrigation sprinkler can spray water is 10 m. What is the largest area of the field that the sprinkler can irrigate?

3. The outer diameter of a DVD is 12 cm and the diameter of the hole at the centre is 1.5 cm. What is the surface area of one side of the DVD?

4.4 Area of a sector

Do you remember this three-coloured spinner? The red part, the yellow part and the blue part are **sectors**.

> The region enclosed by two radii of a circle and the arc between them is a **sector**.

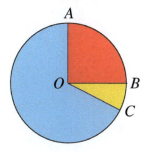

In the diagram on the left, the red, yellow and blue regions are called sector *AOB*, sector *BOC* and sector *AOC*.

A sector is a basic geometric figure, like triangles, quadrilaterals and circles.

Think!

How can you calculate the area of a sector? What is it related to?

> The area of a sector of a circle increases as the angle at the centre of the circle increases.

A circle, with radius r, is like a sector with central angle 360°. Its area is πr^2.

Now suppose you have a sector with central angle 1°. Its area is $\frac{1}{360}\pi r^2$.

Now think about a sector with central angle $n°$.

Its area is $\frac{n}{360}\pi r^2$.

Also, because the arc length of a sector is $l = \frac{n}{180}\pi r$, the area of the sector can be calculated as $\frac{1}{2}lr$.

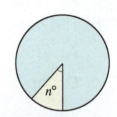

 ## Summary

Given a sector of radius r, central angle $n°$ and arc length l, then:

$$\text{area of sector} = A_{\text{sector}} = \frac{n}{360}\pi r^2 = \frac{1}{2}lr$$

Example 1 In the diagram, the central angle of an extended fan is 135° and the length of a rib of the fan is 30 cm. Find the area of the extended fan.

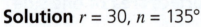

Solution $r = 30$, $n = 135°$

$$A_{\text{sector}} = \frac{n}{360}\pi r^2 = \frac{135}{360} \times 3.14 \times 30^2 = 1059.75$$

The area of the extended fan is 1059.75 cm².

Example 2 The shaded region in the diagram shows the region cleared by a car windscreen wiper. The wiper is fan-shaped and the central angle is 90°. Find the area of the region of windscreen that is cleared by the wiper.

Solution $n = 90$, $r_1 = 40$, $r_2 = 40 - 30 = 10$

$$A = \frac{n}{360}\pi r_1^2 - \frac{n}{360}\pi r_2^2$$

$$= \frac{90}{360} \times 3.14 \times 40^2 - \frac{90}{360} \times 3.14 \times 10^2 = 1177.5$$

The wiper can clear an area of 1177.5 cm².

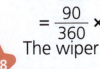

Practice 4.4 (1)

1. Given that the central angle of a sector is 150° and the arc length is 62.8 cm, find the area of the sector.

2. In the diagram, the lengths of the sides of the two connected squares are 8 cm and 3 cm. Find the area of the shaded region.

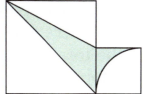

Think!

Emma is on the class sports committee and is planning to organise an outing to watch a sports match. To encourage as many pupils as possible to attend, she carried out a survey to see what sport most pupils would like to see. Her results are shown in the diagram. Based on the information in the diagram, what sport should Emma choose?

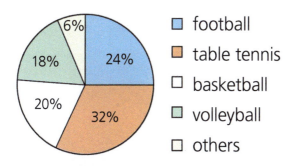

- ☐ football
- ☐ table tennis
- ☐ basketball
- ☐ volleyball
- ☐ others

It looks like I should arrange for us to see a table tennis match.

Talk about it

In the diagram on the right, the circle represents a whole. Which sector represents 25% of the population?

If the whole circle represents a class of 40 pupils, how many pupils are represented by sector *B*?

If the whole circle represents £10 in your pocket, how much money does sector *C* represent?

The two charts above are called **pie charts**, the full circle represents the whole and the sectors represent the different parts of the whole. The size of the sector reflects the percentage of the whole.

Practice 4.4 (2)

1. There were 44 000 chickens, 20 000 ducks and 16 000 geese on a poultry farm this year. What percentages do the chickens, the ducks and the geese represent of the total number of poultry? Show the information in a pie chart.

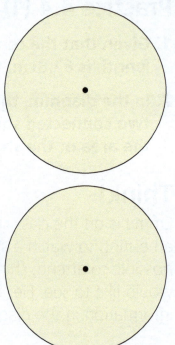

2. Investigate the ambitions of the pupils in your class. Find out what occupations they want to follow, such as engineers, teachers, chefs, doctors. Calculate the percentage for each career. Show the information in a pie chart.

Unit summary

In this unit you have learned about the concepts and formulas for the circumference and area of a circle, the length of an arc and the area of a sector. In practical activities, you have experienced the process of converting new problems into familiar problems that you know how to solve and learned mathematical ideas about transforming a region with curved sides to one with straight sides to approximate areas.

The main contents of this chapter are as follows (complete the formulas):

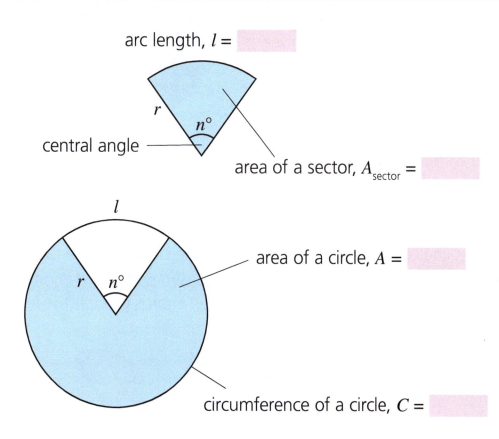

arc length, $l =$

central angle

area of a sector, $A_{sector} =$

area of a circle, $A =$

circumference of a circle, $C =$

In particular, this relationship:

$$\frac{l}{C} = \frac{n}{360} \quad \text{and} \quad \frac{A_{sector}}{A} = \frac{n}{360}$$

So: $\dfrac{l}{C} = \dfrac{A_{sector}}{A}$

Investigation activity: The minimum number of cuts

Dylan is celebrating his birthday. His 28 classmates bought a large round cake for him. After singing 'Happy Birthday' and blowing out the candles, it was time to cut the cake. There is no easy way to divide a round cake into 29 equal pieces. However, Dylan didn't mind about this because he knew that his classmates had not come for the birthday cake, and whether the cake was divided equally was not important. Instead, he wanted to take this opportunity to solve a problem with his classmates. He stipulated that each cut can only be made across the top of the cake. Each cut will divide the cake into two pieces.

What is the smallest number of cuts that would need to be made so that every pupil could get a piece of cake?

The essence of Dylan's problem is: What is the greatest number of pieces of cake that can be produced by using several chords (a chord is a straight line connected by two points on the circumference of the circle)?

We know that any chord cuts a circle into two parts. Two chords can cut the circle into four parts at most, three chords can cut the circle into seven parts at most.

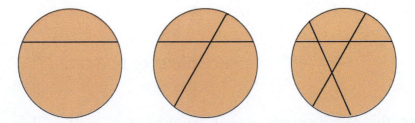

Draw a circle and investigate: How many pieces will four chords produce at most? How many will five chords produce at most? How many will six chords produce at most? What kind of law is behind this activity?

Can you solve Dylan's problem?

Extra reading material: The history of π

Liu Hui was an outstanding mathematician of the Weijin Dynasty in China and one of the founders of ancient Chinese mathematical theory. In the ancient Chinese mathematical masterpiece *The Nine Chapters on the Mathematical Art* he studied what happens if the number of sides of a regular polygon is gradually increased until it approximates the circumference of a circle.

He obtained the approximation for π as $\frac{3927}{1250}$ = 3.1416. This was a very accurate approximation of π.

Liu Hui

Zu Chongzhi

Two hundred years later, Zu Chongzhi, an outstanding mathematician who lived during the Liu Song and Southern Qi Dynasties, achieved a 'circle' with 24 576 sides. Using the same method, he calculated that the circumference : diameter ratio is between 3.141 592 6 and 3.141 592 7.

For ease of use, he used two fractions, $\frac{22}{7}$ and $\frac{355}{113}$, to approximate π. This discovery was made a thousand years earlier than it was in the West.

$\frac{22}{7}$ is called the rate of Yue and $\frac{355}{113}$ is called the rate of Mi.

In order to commemorate Zu Chongzhi, $\frac{355}{113}$ is also known as the rate of Zu.

In 1596, the German mathematician Ludolph van Ceulen discovered a value of π that was accurate to 15 decimal places, and then another that was accurate to 35 decimal places. Historically, the 35-point approximation 3.141 592 653 589 793 238 462 643 383 279 502 88 is called the Ludolph number.

In the late 1940s, American mathematicians calculated the value of π to 808 decimal places, which was the most accurate figure produced by manual calculations.

With the development of the computer, it is now possible to estimate the value of π to a billion decimal places and mathematicians have proved that it is neither an integer nor a fraction, but it is an infinite non-repeating decimal. It is impossible to calculate its accurate value.

Appendix

1.

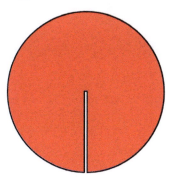 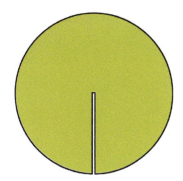 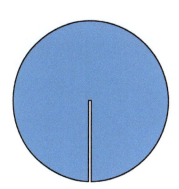

2.

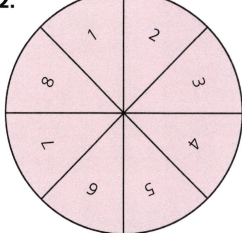 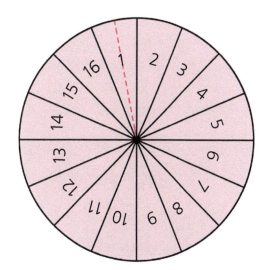

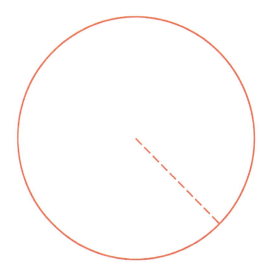 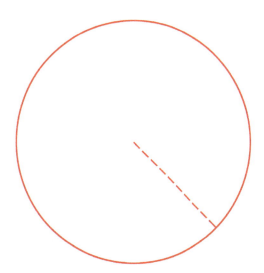